Quantitative Research in
Education

Dedicated to

Anita W. Hoy
Vicky K. Adams
Simply the Best

Quantitative Research in
Education

A Primer

Second Edition

Wayne K. Hoy ● **Curt M. Adams**

The Ohio State University **University of Oklahoma**

Los Angeles | London | New Delhi
Singapore | Washington DC

Los Angeles | London | New Delhi
Singapore | Washington DC

FOR INFORMATION:

SAGE Publications, Inc.
2455 Teller Road
Thousand Oaks, California 91320
E-mail: order@sagepub.com

SAGE Publications Ltd.
1 Oliver's Yard
55 City Road
London EC1Y 1SP
United Kingdom

SAGE Publications India Pvt. Ltd.
B 1/I 1 Mohan Cooperative Industrial Area
Mathura Road, New Delhi 110 044
India

SAGE Publications Asia-Pacific Pte. Ltd.
3 Church Street
#10-04 Samsung Hub
Singapore 049483

Acquisitions Editor: Terri Accomazzo
Editorial Assistant: Georgia McLaughlin
Production Editor: Libby Larson
Copy Editor: Janet Ford
Typesetter: C&M Digitals (P) Ltd.
Proofreader: Alison Syring
Cover Designer: Anupama Krishnan
Marketing Manager: Ashlee Blunk

Printed in the United States of America

Library of Congress Cataloging-in-Publication Data

Hoy, Wayne K.
Quantitative research in education: a primer / Wayne K. Hoy, The Ohio State University, Curt M. Adams, University of Oklahoma.—Second edition.

pages cm
Includes bibliographical references and index.

ISBN 978-1-4833-7641-7 (pbk. : alk. paper)
1. Education—Research—Methodology. 2. Quantitative research. I. Adams, Curt M. II. Title.

LB1028.H69 2015
370.72--dc23   2015006461

15 16 17 18 19 10 9 8 7 6 5 4 3 2 1

BRIEF CONTENTS

DETAILED CONTENTS

SAGE | 50 YEARS

SAGE was founded in 1965 by Sara Miller McCune to support the dissemination of usable knowledge by publishing innovative and high-quality research and teaching content. Today, we publish more than 850 journals, including those of more than 300 learned societies, more than 800 new books per year, and a growing range of library products including archives, data, case studies, reports, and video. SAGE remains majority-owned by our founder, and after Sara's lifetime will become owned by a charitable trust that secures our continued independence.

Los Angeles | London | New Delhi | Singapore | Washington DC

PREFACE

Quantitative Research in Education: A Primer is what the title implies—a beginning overview. Let us slay a few ideological demons and dragons at the outset. We do not believe that there is any one "best" way to conduct research. The appropriate method of research depends on the purpose of the study. Also, there should not be a sharp dichotomy between qualitative and quantitative research; both are valuable and both can be empirical and enlightening. In fact, the two approaches are complementary—not competing. Qualitative researchers are interested in understanding a particular case, exploring new ideas, providing "thick, rich descriptions" of events, and discovering patterns of behavior. Quantitative researchers are concerned with the development and testing of hypotheses, generating models and theories that explain behavior, and generalizing their results across many samples. This text focuses exclusively on quantitative research because it is our primary interest and area of study and because we believe we can give students a good understanding of the research enterprise in a way that stimulates rather than stifles curiosity and creativity.

In recent years, a new term has become part of the academic vocabulary in education: *scientifically based research*. Some are threatened by the term; some see it as negative and counterproductive, whereas others see the term as capturing the essence of educational research. We are not willing to engage in that debate now, but we are on record that research with the following characteristics is good research (National Research Council, 2002):

- It poses significant questions that can be studied empirically.

- It links empirical research to relevant theory.

- It uses methods that enable direct investigation of the research questions.

- It provides a coherent, explicit, and logical chain of reasoning.

- It can be replicated and generalized across studies.

- It is transparent and is reported in order to encourage scrutiny and critique.

These are the principles of sound empirical research in education. Of course, not all studies have all of these attributes, but these principles provide a solid set of goals for sound educational research. In brief, good research in education is empirical, theoretical, and replicable. Students should be convinced of this conclusion by the end of this book.

AIM

The *Primer* is brief and modest—a useful beginning that should enhance understanding and provoke further study. We start with a chapter on the nature of research and science and then turn to the meaning of concepts, variables, and research in education. The goal is to provide sound definitions and meanings illustrated with concrete examples. Of course, it is difficult to understand quantitative research without understanding statistics, and so we examine some of the conceptual foundations of statistics and supply the student with a solid arsenal of elementary statistical tools, with a focus on conceptual understanding rather than technical formulation. Students also need to understand the basic elements of hypotheses and should be able to deconstruct and analyze hypotheses, that is, to understand their structure and substance. Students also must come to know the process of creating their own original hypotheses; to that end, particular strategies and techniques are developed and illustrated, and students are encouraged to practice developing their own theoretically based hypotheses. In the current edition, a concluding chapter has been added to illustrate the practical applications of quantitative research. In each chapter, the abstractions advanced are demonstrated with concrete examples.

Our own experience with students is that too many are put off by quantitative research because they see it as too difficult, too statistical, and too "theoretical." Nothing could be further from the truth. The goal of the *Primer* is to dispel such notions and to generate interest in and understanding of quantitative educational research. The *Primer* distinguishes itself from other texts in that it is brief, conceptual, foundational, user-friendly, and loaded with examples, illustrations, and suggestions for new research.

BASIC APPROACH

Research is creative as well as routine. Its creative dimension is a surprisingly playful weaving of the new with the old. It is probably the routine rather than the necessary rigor of science that is off-putting to new students. And that is understandable. Although there is some joy and satisfaction in creating a resolution to a vexing problem, the exuberance at the new discovery can quickly be dampened by the necessary rigor in testing the novel idea. The spark of creativity can be extinguished by the plodding objectivity of the method.

There is a tension between the creative and the tedious elements of research. Both, however, are important essential ingredients of science. Our goal is to lessen the tension as well as to demonstrate with clarity the creating and testing of explanations. Make no mistake: This book is a primer that should whet the student's appetite for quantitative research. It is neither a comprehensive text on methodology nor a book on statistics, but it should introduce beginning students to both elements in a way that promotes understanding and interest rather than anxiety and boredom.

INTENDED AUDIENCE

This book is written for anyone who wants a quick understanding of the process of scientific inquiry and its utility and who is fascinated with the creation and testing of ideas. Although most of the examples come from education, administration, and psychology, the content and process are the same for all the social and behavioral sciences. Thus, there are many courses where this book can be used. At the master's level, any program that requires a thesis, a research course, or reading of empirical literature would be well-advised to use the *Primer* as a supplement to a course early in the program. At the doctoral level, the book should be used before students engage in their statistics and research sequence. Virtually all EdD and PhD programs require a general course on how to frame and execute a research study for the dissertation; this is another ideal opportunity to use this little book. Just as Strunk and White's *Elements of Style* (2000) is mandatory reading for all undergraduate students, we hope that the *Primer* will become essential reading for all graduate students in education, psychology, sociology, and the other social and behavioral sciences.

CONTENT

Chapter 1 is a brief discussion of the nature of research and science. Four ways of knowing are examined, concluding that the method of science produces the most reliable knowledge because it is systematic, controlled, and empirical. The chapter grapples with the sticky problem of objectivity and suggests that scientific objectivity is a goal, not a characteristic, of researchers. In addition, the tools of research, the meaning of reality, and the nature of theory are explored and illustrated.

Chapter 2 explains the nature of concepts, variables, and research problems. The topics here provide the foundational elements for developing, critiquing, and understanding social science research. Each idea presented in the chapter is illustrated with multiple concrete examples and applications. For example, the concept of organizational structure is defined as a multidimensional construct, with each element carefully delineated. A goal of this chapter is to provide rich conceptual capital for eventual development into original hypotheses. The touchstone of quantitative research is the variable. We explain the transformation of concepts into variables and propose a system for distinguishing between different kinds of variables. In brief, not only are the notions of concepts and variables explained, but multiple examples are used to illustrate the difference between theoretical and operational definitions. Finally, the chapter concludes by defining research problems, providing examples, and challenging students to develop their own research questions.

Chapter 3 examines the conceptual foundation of statistics. The focus is on understanding statistics, not on statistical computation. There are a myriad of statistical packages, such as SPSS (predictive analytics software) or SAS (Statistical Analysis System) that efficiently attend to the calculations; hence, it is the understanding of the statistics that is important, not the computation. The basic statistics include measures of central tendency, measures of variability, and a set of inferential statistical tests— t tests, simple analysis of variance, chi-squares, correlation, multiple regression, and hierarchical linear modeling (HLM). This is a user-friendly chapter that should allay any anxiety that beginning students have with statistics and demonstrate the value of statistics as useful tools.

Chapter 4 analyzes the structure and function of hypotheses. After discussing the characteristics of a good hypothesis, the chapter examines the kinds of hypotheses and the roles they play in research. For example, the analysis distinguishes between substantive and statistical hypotheses and between null and alternative hypotheses. Imposter and misconceived hypotheses are examined, as are tautologies and hypotheses that are unspecified and untestable. We propose a system for analyzing, critiquing, and diagramming hypotheses—in much the same way as English students diagram sentences. In all cases, specific examples illustrate the procedure. By the end of this chapter, students should be expert at diagramming and analyzing hypotheses of all kinds.

Chapter 5 grapples with the question of how original hypotheses are invented. Ideas for new hypotheses are suggested from a variety of sources, including observation, imagination, and published theoretical literature. We explicate the role of theory in the generation of hypotheses and the theoretical arguments that support them and then illustrate with examples. Using concepts from earlier chapters as well as ones developed in this chapter, the student is challenged to be creative in crafting novel hypotheses and framing intriguing research.

Chapter 6 extends the elements of quantitative research with a series of practical examples. We use the concepts of collective trust, organizational climate, and improvement science to illustrate the utility of a quantitative approach. We conclude the chapter with a set of guidelines that steer practitioners to a systematic method of studying and analyzing the problems of practice.

PEDAGOGICAL AIDS TO UNDERSTANDING

Key Terms are highlighted in the text when they first appear and then summarized in a list at the end of the chapter so that students can review the key concepts. Some students may find it valuable to look at the key terms to cue their reading of the chapter.

The Summary for each chapter helps the student review the major ideas and gives an overview; the major ideas are highlighted.

Check Your Understanding is a series of exercises and questions to assess the student's ability to understand, value, and apply the content of the chapter. If you can do the exercises, you have understood the text.

In the Glossary entries, all the key terms in the text are concisely and clearly defined so that students have handy access to terms needing review.

The Diagramming Table, presented in Chapter 4, enables students to diagram and dissect hypotheses in much the same way an English student would diagram a sentence. The table ensures that the key elements of a hypothesis are considered, analyzed, and understood.

"Elements of a Proposal" (Appendix A) gives students specific directions for developing a quantitative research plan. Tips about the introduction, the review of the literature, the generation of hypotheses, and the design and method of the study are sketched. The elements of a proposal are likened to the first three chapters of a thesis or dissertation. The outline motivates students to get started—the most difficult step for many.

"A Few Writing Tips" (Appendix B) gives a number of salient writing suggestions. Over the years in the professorship, we have found that students tend to make the same simple slipups over and over again—mistakes of grammar, usage, voice, agreement in number, and split infinitives. This simple guide does not cover all errors, but it does underscore many common errors students make in formal writing. In fact, it might be a good idea to read Appendix B before starting the book.

ACKNOWLEDGMENTS

We would be remiss if we did not acknowledge our intellectual debt to both W. W. Charters Jr. and Fred Kerlinger. Many of the ideas in the *Primer* come from Charters and Kerlinger. Charters's treatment of research in *On Understanding Variables and Hypotheses in Scientific Research* and Kerlinger's analysis of statistics in *Foundations of Behavioral Research* and his examination of research in *Behavioral Research: A Conceptual Approach* were particularly valuable. We thank Lauren Bailes, George Boszilkov, Ryan Miskell, Jordan Ware, Ellen Dollarhide, and Professors John Tarter and Hsin-Chieh Wu, who read numerous drafts of this text and made editorial as well as substantive suggestions. Four professors field tested the *Primer* with their classes and provided useful feedback: Curt Adams, University of Oklahoma; Michael DiPaola, College of William and Mary; Patrick Forsyth, University of Oklahoma; and C. John Tarter, University of Alabama. Finally, thanks to Professors Richard Lomax and Brian Warnick of The Ohio State University, Gail Schneider of the University of Wisconsin at Milwaukee, Barbara Lacost of the University of Nebraska, Kamair Kouzekanani of Texas A&M University at Corpus Christi, Farzin Madjidi of Pepperdine University, and Megan Tschannen-Moran of the College of William and Mary.

In this second edition of the *Quantitative Research in Education: A Primer*, Curt Adams of the University of Oklahoma joined the writing team and did major work in revising the book. We added a chapter on practical applications of quantitative analysis, expanded the number of statistical analyses, and refreshed examples throughout the text. We tried to keep the volume to minimum size by deleting materials as we added others. We believe a primer should be modest in length, clear and precise in explication, conceptual rather than technical, and friendly and fascinating. The reader will be the judge as to how well we succeeded. Although we had much help from students and colleagues, any mistakes or misconceptions are ours.

W. K. H.
Naples, FL

C. M. A.
Tulsa, OK

1

THE NATURE OF RESEARCH AND SCIENCE

There are two major approaches to research in the behavioral and social sciences—qualitative and quantitative. **Qualitative research** focuses on in-depth understanding of social and human behavior and the reasons behind such behavior. The qualitative method depends on the reported experiences of individuals through ethnographic analyses, fieldwork, and case studies. **Quantitative research** is scientific investigation that includes both experiments and other systematic methods that emphasize control and quantified measures of performance (Proctor & Capaldi, 2006). Measurement and statistics are central to quantitative research because they are the connections between **empirical** observation and mathematical expressions of relations. Qualitative researchers are interested in understanding, exploring new ideas, and discovering patterns of behavior. Quantitative researchers are concerned with the development and testing of **hypotheses** and the generation of models and theories that explain behavior. The two approaches are complementary, but this book is primarily about quantitative research.

WAYS OF KNOWING

The philosopher Charles Peirce has proposed four basic ways of knowing—(1) the method of tenacity, (2) the method of authority, (3) the method of intuition, and (4) the method of science (Buchler, 1955). Let's take a look at each.

The **method of tenacity** refers to the fact that people hold to certain beliefs because they have always known these beliefs to be true. Habit is strong. Once people believe in something, they look for evidence to confirm that belief and ignore disconfirming instances. They repeat beliefs over and over and in the process convince themselves of the correctness of their perspective. Even in the face of clear facts to the contrary, they hold tenaciously to their beliefs and build new knowledge from **assumptions** that are often false.

The **method of authority** is anchored in the statements of experts and is the second way of knowing. If an idea has public support, it must be true. Individuals turn to those in authority positions for truth; they turn to the church, their leaders, their superiors, and experts. Peirce suggests that the method of authority is superior to the method of tenacity because human progress can be made, albeit slowly, by using this method. Authority seems to be a necessary condition for social life. Groups bestow legitimate power to those in authority positions; that is, the group legitimizes the belief that those in authority have not only the right, but also the obligation to guide others. The method of authority is not necessarily unsound, but it is clearly not always sound (Kerlinger, 1986).

The **method of intuition** is built on assumptions that are obvious; such propositions are accepted as self-evident. They may agree with reason, but not necessarily with experience. The idea seems to be that individuals can discover the truth by using reason and logic because there is a natural inclination toward truth. But, as Fred Kerlinger (1986) points out, "Whose reason?" Suppose two sincere people use reason, but come to opposite conclusions. Who is right? Is it a matter of taste? Is something that is evident to many people correct? Not always. We now know the world is round, not flat, even though the flat world was self-evident to people for centuries. The test of the method of intuition is that the issue in question is "self-evident" and just "stands to reason." Unfortunately, many self-evident propositions are simply not true.

The method of science, or **reflective inquiry**, is the fourth way of knowing or fixing belief. To Peirce and to scientists in general, it is the most **reliable** way of knowing. Peirce argues that the method of science provides a means to fix beliefs in such a way that the "ultimate conclusion of every man must be the same. . . . There are real things, whose characters are entirely independent of opinions about them" (Buchler, 1955, p. 18; see also Boghossian, 2006). The **scientific approach** has two unique characteristics absent in the other methods of knowing. **Science** is self-critical and self-correcting. These safeguards are so conceived to control and verify the procedures and experiments and produce dependable outcomes. Even if a hypothesis is supported, the researcher is skeptical and seeks rival hypotheses in an attempt to find counter examples and refine the findings.

When using the scientific approach, no explanation is final, because a better one may be devised at any time; science is open. Nothing is irrevocably proved; in fact, those with a scientific temper stay clear of the term *proved* when talking about findings in educational or psychological research; instead, they are content with the statement "At this time, the weight of the evidence supports this conclusion." The norms of science are oriented toward openness, transparency, and public inspection.

Peirce argues that safeguards and built-in checks of the scientific approach are outside the scientist's personal attitudes, values, perceptions, and emotions; that is, the procedures of science are outside the scientists themselves. We agree with Kerlinger (1986) that such an impersonal, disinterested, and external perspective is best captured in one word—**objectivity**. The ideal of objectivity coupled with rigorous and controlled empirical tests leads to dependable knowledge and promotes confidence in the outcomes.

OBJECTIVITY

Before proceeding, we return to the notion of objectivity because it is so important to science and a scientific approach. Although it may not be possible to attain complete objectivity, it is the aim of the scientist; it is the ideal to which researchers and scientists are committed. Objectivity *is impartial judgment that rests outside an individual's personal preferences, biases, and wishes* (Peirce as cited in Buchler, 1955). Admittedly, attaining this is no easy task, yet it is the goal to which scientists adhere—to find a method of fixing beliefs that is independent of our desires and wills, that is outside or apart from ourselves, as Peirce would say. Scientists try to design their experiments such that they are apart from themselves, their influence, their predilections, and their biases. They objectify their ideas, that is, make them **objects** that have a separate existence from the researcher and can be tested in an independent fashion.

Although it is true that all knowledge is affected and at times distorted by the prejudices and predispositions of observers, the goal is to find a method of knowing that stands the test of independence from the researcher—in other words, one that is objective. Kerlinger (1979) defines objectivity as *agreement among knowledgeable judges of what is observed and what is done* and asserts that the main condition of objectivity "is ideally, that *any* observers with minimum competence will agree on their observations" (p. 9). In education and educational administration, we use objective measures of our **concepts**. They are called objective because with clear instructions, individuals score the measures and get the same results (within small margins of error).

A second and wider notion of objectivity in educational research is the attempt by researchers to make their designs and procedures so clear and exact that others can replicate their studies to get the same or similar findings (Kerlinger, 1979). When educational researchers carry out their studies, they aim for objectivity by making their procedures, measures, and controls clear, explicit, and replicable. Replication is an indispensable feature of a scientific approach that is objective. Make no mistake, it is easier to be objective in the physical sciences than in the social sciences because the physical is more amenable to objectification than the social. Furthermore, in education **variables,** such as leadership, creativity, school effectiveness, school climate, empowerment, and trust are more complex, more problematical, and harder to isolate from other variables. The bottom line is that objectivity in the social sciences is more difficult; hence, educational research is less objective than in the physical sciences. Although objectivity is more difficult to achieve in education, it is certainly not impossible, and it is the goal. Moreover, the principle, the approach, and the general methods of objectivity are the same whether the objects of study are physical, individual, or social.

Finally, *objectivity* as it is used here is *not a characteristic* of individual researchers; rather, it is a description of a procedure (Kerlinger, 1979). Although some people may be more objective than others, *objectivity* as it is used here and in science refers to the approach and method of science and not to the individual scientists themselves. In sum, objectivity is a goal of all science; it is a disinterested, impartial, and external perspective and a set of procedures that enables observers with minimum competence to agree on their observations. Objective procedures are clear, accurate, consistent, replicable, and reliable.

THE NATURE OF SCIENCE

The purpose of all science is to understand the world in which we live and work. Scientists describe what they see, discover regularities, and formulate theories (Babbie, 1990). **Organizational science**, for example, attempts to describe and explain regularities in the behavior of individuals and groups within organizations. Organizational scientists seek basic principles that provide a general understanding of the structure and dynamics of organizational life, a relatively recent goal in educational administration (Roberts, Hulin, & Rousseau, 1978).

Some researchers view science as a static, interconnected set of principles that explains the universe in which we live, but most would agree that science is not inert. **Science** *is a dynamic process of experimentation and observation that produces an interconnected set of principles, which in turn generates further experimentation, and observation, and refinement* (Conant, 1951). In this view, the basic aim of science is to find general explanations, called "theories." Scientific theories are created by thoughtful individuals trying to understand and explain how things work. Good theories are explanations that are heuristic; they predict novel observations (Wright, 2013). No **theory** (explanation), however, is ever taken as final because a better one may be devised at any time as new data become available.

The Empirical Nature of Science

At the heart of our working definition of science is experimentation and observation. These are critical tools of science, and they are linked to an empirical approach. *Empirical* refers to evidence based on observations, especially evidence obtained by systematic and controlled **scientific research** (Kerlinger, 1979). In other words, the empirical evidence in science is based on experimentation and careful observations, which are methodical, measured, and controlled. Science is an empirical approach to knowledge; scientific knowledge is based on systematic and controlled studies of hypothetical explanations.

Carefully obtained empirical evidence provides a check on unbridled assertions about the world, assertions that may or may not be true (Kerlinger, 1986). The frequent comment "That is an empirical question" refers to the need for an empirical test of the assertion. Where is the empirical evidence that supports the conclusion? Researchers and scientists are much more confident when their conclusions are based on empirical evidence rather than tradition, intuition, authority, or religious or political beliefs. In brief, at the heart of science is empirical evidence.

Scientific Tools

Researchers use statistics as a tool to test their observations and findings. **Inferential statistics** provide a mathematical way to see if the results are likely a function of chance. Did these results of this experiment occur by chance, or is some systematic influence producing the outcomes? That is the question that inferential statistics answer. Scientists use statistics and probability to reject the chance model and support their theoretical explanation.

Deduction is a logical method of deriving specific predictions and hypotheses from a general set of assumptions, that is, moving from general premises to specific predictions and conclusions. Consider the assumption that *a threat to one's status leads individuals to respond in ways that enable them to gain control over the threat.* Apply this premise to teachers. Not surprisingly, teachers want to minimize student threat to their status as teacher and maintain control over students. Teachers typically dress in more formal attire than their students; they usually insist on the use of formal address by students (e.g., Mr. Smith); they correct students for not behaving; they give verbal reprimands to students for not following their directives; and they send unruly students to the principal's office for discipline. The premise and supporting evidence suggest the following hypothesis: *The more threatened a teacher's status by students, the more likely the teacher responds with an autocratic approach to control* (Hoy, 2001). Deduction does not go beyond its basic premise; it simply conserves the premise.

Induction is another logical method used by scientists and researchers. Here, the researcher moves from a series of observations in a variety of situations to a **generalization** that captures the basic tendencies in the observations. In other words, a generalization is developed from a set of specific instances. Of course, induction does not prove anything, but it leads to generalizations that can be tested.

Both deduction and induction are useful scientific tools. Yet, there is a third logical process that is not as widely known, but that also has scientific utility. **Abduction** is the process of studying a number of phenomena, observing their pattern, and formulating a causal hypothesis (Peirce, 1940). Proctor and Capaldi (2006) explain that abduction is neither induction nor deduction. It is not induction because there may only be a few examples and the generalization is not about their shared **properties,** but rather about their cause. Deduction is not involved because the generalization is not derived from the phenomena it applies to, but is rather an explanation of them.

The point here is that scientists use many methods to develop and test their explanations. Statistics, deduction, induction, and abduction are useful tools, yet none of them alone is sufficient. These methods must be harnessed to a scientific approach that is grounded in empirical evidence developed from careful, systematic, and controlled research. One final observation—science has two faces: (1) the creative formulation of ideas and explanation (developing hypotheses), and (2) the rigorous, systematic testing of ideas and explanations (testing hypotheses).

THE SCIENTIFIC APPROACH

The scientific approach is a process of reflective inquiry, which is described in general form in John Dewey's (1933) classic analysis *How We Think*. The approach has four basic steps:

1. The identification and definition of a problem (Problem)

2. The formulation of a hypothesis to solve the problem (Hypothesis)

3. The logical analysis of the implications of the hypothesis (Reasoning)

4. Testing to corroborate or reject the hypothesis (Testing)

Whether the objective is problem solving, decision making, or scientific research, the reflective process is the same. Of course, its application is more or less rigorous, depending on the situation. For example, in real-life decision making the reflection is often truncated because of the constraints of time and resources, whereas in **experimental research** we see a rigorous application of the approach. Let's turn to each step in the reflective process to get a better sense of the scientific approach (see "Elements of a Proposal," Appendix A).

Problem

A problem, obstacle, or new idea triggers the reflective process of inquiry (see "Elements of a Proposal," Appendix A). This stage of the approach is often filled with struggle and angst; the individual grapples with a difficulty, which may be vague and sketchy at best, as an attempt is made to understand the issues and complexities at hand. Just what is the problem? How can one express it? What are its dimensions? How complex is it? How does one conceptualize the difficulties? The challenge is to wrap your mind around the problem as you begin to analyze and specify it. This may be the most important step in the process because framing the problem has a great deal to do with the paths to a solution. A scientist usually needs a reasonable formulation of a problem before proceeding. To a researcher, a **research problem** is a question, which is carefully stated and guides the research. Of course, reframing or refining the initial problem is likely as more information and data become available. Remember, science is a dynamic process, not a static one; ideas beget other ideas; more data create new questions.

Hypothesis

After conceptualizing the problem, the scientist proposes provisional answers to the question. In the process of generating answers, scientists draw on their knowledge, experience, observations, and imagination to formulate tentative responses to the issues. A possible solution to the puzzle is their hypothesis—a conjectural statement that indicates the relation between key ideas in their formulation of an answer. Often the hypothesis takes the form of "If x, then y; that is, if such and such occurs, then the consequences will be so and so." The development of hypotheses is a creative journey based on experience, observations, reflection, or some implicit or explicit theory (plausible explanation). The formulation of hypotheses is the creative side of the scientific approach. The inventive researcher proposes novel explanations and insightful hypotheses.

Reasoning

At this stage of the process, the scientist deduces the consequences of the hypotheses. What are the outcomes and implications if this hypothesis is true? At an informal level, the process demonstrates how ongoing experience leads to re-approximations of answers through inquiry. The process of deduction often leads to a reformulation of the problem and hypotheses because things don't work out for one reason or another. For example, the scientist may have overlooked an important element or miscalculated or simply finds it impossible to test the relation. At this stage, the reasoning is deductive, trying to anticipate the consequences of a given generalization (hypothesis). Dewey focused on the deductive aspect of the reasoning, but once the deduction leads to other difficulties, individuals may draw on other reasoning tools—induction and abduction. For example, looking for regularities in data and formulating possible causes of those patterns may provide insight and allow for reframing of the problem, and the generation of new hypotheses. Likewise, the reasoning may lead to the development of rival hypotheses (see "A Few Writing Tips," Appendix B).

Logical reasoning may also change the question. For instance, in the analysis we may realize that the initial formulation was only a specific instance of a much broader problem. Does programmed instruction improve student achievement in mathematics? This formulation of the problem is probably too narrow because it neglects the *why* question. Why would programmed instruction be effective? We can generalize the problem to the broader and more inclusive form: Does immediate reinforcement lead to more effective learning? Note that the latter question subsumes the former and begins to deal with the causal question. The point is that reasoning can reaffirm the utility of a hypothesis, or it can refine the hypothesis and deal with a more important problem, one that promotes a deeper understanding of the issue. The reasoning process is usually anchored in one's experience or flows from some theoretical explanation.

Testing

The next phase of the process involves making observations, testing, and experimenting; this is the systematic, controlled side of science. Once the problem has been clearly stated, the hypotheses formulated, and the consequences of the hypotheses carefully examined, then the next step is to test the hypotheses. This testing phase involves making observations and devising an experiment or a plan for testing. The plan is an empirical test of the relation expressed in the hypothesis. An important aspect of the testing process is control: We want to control the influence of as many other variables as we can that may affect our relation (hypothesis) so that after the test we have confidence that the relation in question is a viable one. Control in the testing enhances confidence in the outcomes. On the basis of the empirical evidence, the hypothesis is either supported or rejected. The evidence is considered in light of the original problem, and the question is answered, changed, or refined based on the evidence.

Dewey emphasized that the scientific process is not fixed. Depending on the problem and data, the researcher may jump around a bit and use the steps in an order different from the one we just outlined. After the hypothesis is constructed, for instance, the researcher may go back to the problem and revise or reframe it, or as the data are gathered, new ideas and issues may arise, calling for change. The reflective process is neither a neat, simple straight line nor a locked-step procedure; the scientist or researcher often moves spontaneously in a number of directions, jumping forward, skipping steps, then retreating, and then beginning again. Kerlinger (1986) captures the chief feature of the scientific process when he concludes that research may be orderly or disorderly. It does not matter, but what does matter is the controlled rationality of the scientific approach as a progression of reflective inquiry, the interdependence of the parts of the method, and the principal importance of the problem and its statement.

THEORY: A SCIENTIFIC CONCEPT

Theory is one of those words that makes many people uncomfortable, largely because of their misconceptions of the term. Much of the skepticism about theory is based on the assumption that education in general, and educational administration in particular, is art, not science, a skepticism that has plagued all social sciences. Theory in the natural sciences, on the other hand, has attained respectability not only because it necessarily involves precise description, but also because it describes ideal phenomena that "work" in practical applications.

Most people think that scientists deal with facts, whereas philosophers delve into theory. Indeed, to many individuals, including educators and educational administrators, *facts* and *theories* are antonyms; that is, facts are real and their meanings self-evident, whereas theories are speculations or dreams. Theory in education, however, has the same role as theory in physics, chemistry, biology, or psychology—that is, providing general explanations and guiding research.

Theory Defined

As the ultimate aim of science, *theory* has acquired a variety of definitions. Some early agreement, for example, emerged in the field of educational administration that the definition of theory produced by Herbert Feigl (1951) was an adequate starting point. Feigl defined *theory* as a set of assumptions from which a larger set of empirical laws can be derived by purely logico-mathematical procedures. Although there was much initial support for this definition, Donald Willower (1975) cautioned that Feigl's definition was so rigorous as to exclude most theory in education and educational administration. A more general and useful definition for the social sciences was provided by Kerlinger (1986): "A theory is a set of interrelated **constructs** (concepts), definitions, and propositions that present a systematic view of phenomena by specifying relations among variables, with the purpose of explaining and predicting phenomena" (p. 9). Willower's (1975) definition is more parsimonious: He defined theory simply as a body of interrelated, consistent generalizations that explain phenomena.

In the study of education, the following definition of theory is useful: Theory *is a set of interrelated concepts, definitions, assumptions, and generalizations that systematically describes and explains regularities in behavior in educational organizations.* Moreover, hypotheses are derived from the theory to predict additional relations among the concepts. When the hypotheses receive overwhelming empirical support, the accepted hypotheses become principles (Hoy & Miskel, 2013). This definition suggests three things:

1. First, theory is logically composed of concepts, definitions, assumptions, and generalizations.

2. Second, the major function of theory is to describe and explain—in fact, theory is a general explanation, which often leads to basic principles.

3. Third, theory is heuristic because it stimulates and guides the further development of knowledge.

Theories are by nature general and abstract; they are not strictly true or false, but rather they are either useful or not useful. They are useful to the extent that they generate explanations that help us understand more easily. Albert Einstein, one of the greatest theorists of all times, and Leopold Infeld (Einstein & Infeld, 1966) capture the essence of theorizing in the following:

> In our endeavor to understand reality we are somewhat like a man trying to understand the mechanism of a closed watch. He sees the face and the moving hands, even hears its ticking, but he has no way of opening the case. If he is ingenious he may form some picture of a mechanism, which could be responsible for all the things he observes, but he may never be quite sure his picture is the only one which could explain his observations. He will never be able to compare his picture with the real mechanism, and he cannot even imagine the possibility of the meaning of such a comparison. (p. 31)

In sum, theory is a special language that explains and helps us understand some phenomenon, for example, learning, motivation, or administration (Tosi, 2009). Just as with any language, theory has its vocabulary (concepts) and grammar (generalizations). Concepts are abstract words that are given specific definitions, which enable us to agree on the meaning of the terms. Words alone, however, are not sufficient to explain something. We need to know not only the meaning of the words, but also why and how they relate to each other. In other words, we need to combine our concepts into coherent generalizations that indicate the relation between two or more concepts. For example, "division of labor produces specialization," and "specialization creates expertise." Note that these two theoretical generalizations each indicate the relation between two concepts, and together they yield an explanation of how expertise can be developed in organizations. In brief, theories provide explanations; they provide a coherent and connected story about why acts, events, and behavior occur (Higgins, 2004; McKinley, 2010).

Meaning of Reality

Reality exists, but our knowledge of it always remains elusive and uncertain. It should not be surprising that different individuals often draw different conclusions from the same perceptual experiences because they hold different theories that affect their interpretation of events (Carey & Smith, 1993). Our knowledge consists of our theories, but the form of the theory is less important than the degree to which it generates useful understanding; theory is judged by its utility.

The use of theory in organizational analysis seems indispensable to reflective practice. The beginning student of education may ask, "Do these theories and models really exist?" Our position is the same as Mintzberg's (1989). The models, theories, and configurations used to describe organizations in this book are mere words and pictures on pages, not reality itself. Actual organizations are much more complex than any of these representations: In fact, our conceptual frameworks are simplifications of organizations that underscore some features and neglect others. Hence, they distort reality. The problem is that in many areas we cannot get by without theoretical guidance (implicit, if not explicit, theories), much as a traveler cannot effectively navigate unknown territory without a map.

Our choice is not usually between reality and theory, but rather between alternative theories. Mintzberg (1989) captures the dilemma nicely:

> No one carries reality around in his or her head, no head is that big. Instead we carry around impressions of reality, which amount to implicit theories. Sometimes these are supplemented with explicit frameworks for identifying the concepts and interrelating them—in other words, with formal theories, built on systematic investigation known as research, or at least on systematic consideration of experience. In fact, some phenomena cannot be comprehended without such formal aid—how is one to develop an implicit theory of nuclear fission, for example? (p. 259)

In sum, we all use theories to guide our actions. Some are implicit, and others are explicit; in fact, many of our personal implicit theories are formal ones that have been internalized. To paraphrase John Maynard Keynes (1936), educators who believe themselves to be exempt from any theoretical influences are usually slaves of some defunct theory. Good theories and models exist; they exist where all useful knowledge must survive—in our minds.

COMPONENTS OF THEORY

The nature of theory can be better understood by looking at the meanings of each of the components of theory and how they are related to one another.

Concepts and Constructs

The terms *concept* and *construct* are often used interchangeably. Sociologists are more apt to use *concept*, whereas psychologists typically favor the word *construct*. Both refer to *a term that has been given an abstract, generalized meaning*. A few examples of concepts in sociology are status, social system, stratification, social structure, and culture. Some constructs from psychology are motivation, ego, hostility, personality, and intelligence. In administration, our concepts or constructs include centralization, formalization, leadership, morale, and informal organization. Social scientists invent concepts to help them study and systematically analyze phenomena. In other words, they invent a language to describe behavior. There are at least two important advantages of defining theoretical concepts—first, theorists, researchers, and practitioners can agree on their meaning, and second, their abstractness enhances the development of generalizations.

Although concepts are by definition abstract, there are different levels of abstraction. Examples of terms arranged along a concrete to abstract continuum are *Jefferson Elementary School*, *school*, *service organization*, *organization*, *social system*, and *system*. Each succeeding term is more general and abstract. Generally speaking, terms that are specific to a particular time or place are concrete and less useful in developing theories. The most useful concepts, generalizations, and theories in the social sciences are in the "middle range"; that is, they are somewhat limited in scope rather than all-embracing. For example, organizational theories are not attempts to summarize all we know about organizations; rather, they explain some of the consistencies found in organizations; in our case, schools are of particular interest.

A concept or construct can be defined in at least two ways. First, it may be defined in terms of other words or concepts. For instance, we might define *permissiveness* as the degree to which a teacher employs a relaxed mode of pupil control; that is, *permissiveness* is defined in terms of *relaxedness*, another term that we believe brings more clarity to the concept. Although this kind of definition often provides one with a better understanding of the term, it is inadequate from a scientific point of view. The researcher must be able to define the concept in measurable terms. *A set of operations or behaviors that has been used to measure a concept is its* **operational definition**. For example, an operational definition of permissiveness might be the number of hall passes a teacher issues per day. This definition is limited, clear, and concise. Permissiveness is the specific set of operations measured. The intelligence quotient (IQ) is the standard operational definition of intelligence, and leadership can be measured and operationalized using Bass's Multi-factor Leadership Questionnaire (1998). Operationalism mandates that the procedures involved in the relation between the observer and the measures for observing be explicitly stated so that they can be duplicated by any other equally trained researcher (Dubin, 1969). Remember that objectivity is a pivotal part of science and research.

Assumptions and Generalizations

An assumption is a statement that is taken for granted or accepted as true. Assumptions accepted without proof are often, but not necessarily, self-evident. For example, consider the following assumptions:

1. There is no one best way to teach.

2. All ways of teaching are not equally effective.

The first assumption challenges the conventional idea that there are universal principles for effective teaching regardless of time or place. The second assumption challenges the notion that the complexity of teaching makes it futile to seek guiding principles. Now consider a third assumption:

3. The best way to teach depends on the nature of the teaching task.

The third assumption posits that effective teaching is conditional; it depends on the nature of the teaching task. All these assumptions have been accepted as reasonable by various groups of people; in fact, there is evidence that all three assumptions might lead to an explanation of effective teaching.

A generalization is a statement or proposition that indicates the relation of two or more concepts or constructs. In other words, a generalization links concepts in a meaningful fashion. Many kinds of generalizations are found in theoretical formulations:

- *Assumptions* are generalizations if they specify the relationship among two or more concepts.

- *Hypotheses* are generalizations with limited empirical support.

- *Principles* are generalizations with substantial empirical support.

- *Laws* are generalizations with an overwhelming degree of empirical support (more than principles); there are few laws in the social sciences, but consider the law of supply and demand in economics.

The basic form of knowledge in all disciplines is similar; it consists of concepts or constructs, generalizations, and theories, each dependent on the one preceding it. Figure 1.1 summarizes the basic components of theory that are necessary for the development of knowledge. The figure shows that concepts are eventually linked together into generalizations that in turn form a logically consistent set of propositions providing a general explanation of a phenomenon (a theory). The theory is then empirically checked by the development and testing of hypotheses deduced from the theory. The results of the research then provide the data for accepting, rejecting, reformulating, or refining and clarifying the basic generalizations of the theory. Over time, with continued empirical support and evidence, the generalizations develop into principles that explain the phenomenon. In the case of organizational theory, principles are developed to explain the structure and dynamics of organizations and the role of the individual in organizations. Theory is both the beginning and the end of scientific research. It serves as the basis for generating hypotheses to test propositions that explain observable empirical phenomena, but in the end it also provides the general explanations and knowledge of a field.

THE NATURE OF SCIENTIFIC RESEARCH

Research is inextricably related to theory; therefore, many of the misconceptions and ambiguities surrounding theory are reflected in the interpretation of the meaning and purpose of research. Some individuals use the term *research* loosely—for example, going to the library to review some literature and draw some conclusion. We use the term in a more rigorous scientific fashion, one that is consistent with a scientific approach. Research is systematic, empirical investigation to test theory and gain a general understanding of some phenomenon. Kerlinger (1986) provides us with a more formal definition: "Scientific research is systematic, controlled, empirical, and critical investigation of hypothetical propositions about the presumed relations among natural phenomena" (p. 10).

Figure 1.1 Theory: Its Components and Testing

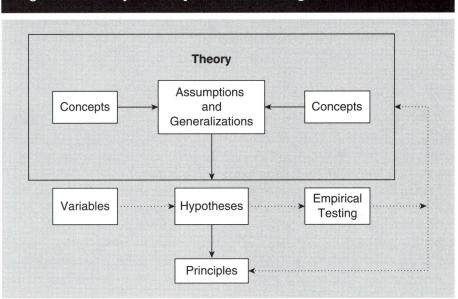

Source: www.waynekhoy.com/pdfs/Theory-Research.pdf. © Hoy, 2007

This definition suggests that scientific research is guided by hypotheses, which are empirically checked against observations about reality in a systematic and controlled way. The observations are systematic and controlled to prevent spurious conclusions. Many school variables (e.g., leadership, school climate, teaching style) are positively correlated with student achievement, but once the socioeconomic level of the school is considered, the positive relationship disappears; thus, variables like socioeconomic level must be controlled in such studies of school achievement. Furthermore, evidence to test hypotheses is based on objective and empirical data subjected to disciplined inquiry. Finally, the results of such tests are then open to public scrutiny and critical analyses by other scientists and researchers.

Good research in education is theoretical, empirical, controlled, and replicable. Haphazard observations followed by the conclusion that the facts speak for themselves do not qualify as scientific research; in fact, such unrefined empiricism can distort reality and does not lead to the systematic development of knowledge (Hoy & Miskel, 2008). Well-conceived surveys and ethnographic studies for the express purpose of developing hypotheses are at times useful starting points in terms of hypothesis and theory generation; ultimately, however, knowledge in any discipline is expanded by research that is guided by hypotheses that are derived from theory. In brief, findings from research are not as important as the general patterns and explanations that they provide.

TYPES OF QUANTITATIVE RESEARCH

There are different types of research; for example, we have already distinguished between quantitative and qualitative research. We turn to some of the common distinctions of quantitative research that are found in the literature.

Experimental and Nonexperimental (or Ex Post Facto) Research

One useful distinction for our purposes is to differentiate between experimental and nonexperimental (or ex post facto) research. Many people think that all quantitative research is experimental. Not true! In fact, most research in education, and in the behavioral and social sciences for that matter, is **nonexperimental research**. Experimental research is the ideal because there is more control over the factors that might confound the findings. But, experimental research is difficult to conduct in educational settings because parents don't want their children involved in experiments; furthermore, this research requires more control over things than most educators have at their disposal. Experimental research is more easily conducted in a laboratory rather than in a social setting.

To conduct an experiment, the researcher has to be able to manipulate one specific aspect of the situation called the **independent variable** (more about variables in Chapter 2). Ideally, a number of conditions must be met to have a good experiment:

- Subjects should be selected at random.

- Then the subjects should be assigned to groups at random.

- Next, the experimental and control groups should be selected at random.

- Finally, the researcher must manipulate the independent variable, that is, apply an intervention or treatment to the experimental groups and withhold treatment from the control group.

In sum, experimental research is systematic empirical inquiry where the researcher introduces changes, notes effects, and has full control over the design of the study.

In nonexperimental or **ex post facto research**, the situation cannot be manipulated because the change in the independent variable has already occurred. For example, a study of school climate typically involves measuring the property in existing schools and not manipulating the climate to produce the wanted type. Nonexperimental research *is systematic empirical inquiry in which the researcher does not have direct control of the independent variable because the variable has already occurred* (Kerlinger, 1986). The basic difference between experimental and nonexperimental research can be summed up in one word—*control*.

Theoretical and Practical Research

Some individuals like to distinguish between what they call practical and theoretical research. This distinction is not useful and is artificial because, in the end, sound theoretical research is practical research. More than a half century ago, the father of modern social psychology, Kurt Lewin (1952), captured the idea in this way, "There is nothing more practical than a good theory" (p. 152). Principles and generalizations that explain how things work are about as practical as it gets!

Descriptive Research

Descriptive research is another phrase that is used to characterize inquiry in the social sciences. It is a term that I typically avoid because it has several connotations, one of which is not really research. Research always should involve examining relations between at least two variables. Yet, many "researchers" simply use statistics to describe the characteristics of various groups of individuals. For example, they ask what the proportions are of males and females in a given group of teachers, the average age and experience of the group, the number who have BA, MA, and PhD degrees, the percentage of teachers who drop out of teaching after one year, the average level of experience before teachers become principals, and on and on. The answers to such queries may be quite useful, but such compilations are not examples of descriptive research because they do not relate variables—a more appropriate term for the process is *social bookkeeping*, not *research*.

Descriptive research is the process of simply describing relations without speculating about the cause. The two variables go together; they are correlated. For example, weight and height are correlated, but gaining weight does not cause you to grow taller. Likewise, growing taller does not necessarily lead to growing heavier. Correlational studies give us interesting information about relations, but until we can begin to make causal inferences, their utility is limited. Careful description is important, but it is only the beginning of the study of causal relations.

SUMMARY

This chapter provides an overview of the nature of research and science. The following propositions are key:

- This text is an analysis of quantitative research; our concern is with reflective inquiry, a scientific approach to understanding.

- Our perspective emphasizes objectivity, empirical data, and theory—a system of concepts, assumptions, and propositions that provide an explanation of the issue at hand.

- Science is a dynamic process of experimentation and observation that produces an interconnected set of principles that in turn generates further experimentation, observation, and refinement.

- Throughout this book, we focus on the critique and generation of hypotheses as well as their systematic, controlled, empirical, and critical investigation.

- Our philosophic stance is eclectic: realistic, pragmatic, and postpositive.

- Finally, our quest is for general patterns and reliable explanations that are supported by rigorous empirical research.

CHECK YOUR UNDERSTANDING

1. Discuss the similarities and differences between "common sense" and "reflective inquiry." In which do you have more confidence and why?

2. Describe an objective measure of organizational structure. What makes the measure objective? To what extent is subjectivity involved in your measure?

3. Discuss the differences among deduction, induction, and abduction.

4. Select a concept or construct in education (e.g., classroom climate, teaching style, school climate). Define your concept in two ways: theoretically (in words) and operationally (as a set of operations).

5. Identify a generalization from the research in education in which you have confidence. What are the concepts in this generalization? Can you define each concept? Can you think of a circumstance when the generalization might not hold?

6. Give a specific example of a hypothesis. How many concepts does the hypothesis contain and what are they? Can the concepts be measured?

7. Discuss the relationship of theory and explanation. What form does scientific explanation take?

KEY TERMS

Abduction (p. 6)

Assumption (p. 1)

Concept (p. 3)

Construct (p. 9)

Deduction (p. 5)

Descriptive
   research (p. 17)

Empirical (p. 1)

Experimental
   research (p. 7)

Ex post facto
   research (p. 16)

Generalization (p. 6)

Hypothesis (p. 1)

Independent
   variable (p. 16)

Induction (p. 6)

Inferential
   statistics (p. 5)

Method of authority (p. 1)

Method of intuition (p. 1)

Method of science (p. 1)

Method of tenacity (p. 1)

Nonexperimental
   research (p. 16)

Objectivity (p. 3)

Objects (p. 3)

Operational
   definition (p. 13)

Organizational
   science (p. 4)

Properties (p. 6)

Qualitative
   research (p. 1)

Quantitative
   research (p. 1)

Reflective inquiry (p. 2)

Reliable (p. 2)

Research problem (p. 7)

Science (p. 2)

Scientific approach (p. 2)

Scientific research (p. 5)

Theory (p. 4)

Variable (p. 4)

2

CONCEPTS, VARIABLES, AND RESEARCH PROBLEMS

In this chapter, we continue to build the ideas and concepts that are necessary for you to plan and conduct quantitative research. To that end, we look at some examples of concepts and the operations that transform them into variables. We examine different kinds of variables and the roles that they play in research, and we conclude with a discussion and examples of research problems.

CONCEPTS

We have already provided you with a working definition of concepts and constructs, terms that we use interchangeably in this text. Both refer to abstractions that have been given specific definitions. Let's look at some examples of organizational concepts and constructs.

Organizational Structure: Bureaucracy

- *Hierarchy of authority* is the extent to which positions or offices are under the control and supervision of a higher office.

- *Division of labor* is the extent to which the work task is divided into specialized work.

- *Impersonality* is the degree to which an organization makes decisions on the basis of facts, unencumbered by personal bias and favoritism.

- *Formalization* is the extent to which organizational procedures are codified. There are set ways to respond to routine decisions.

- *Career perspective* is the extent to which an organization encourages employees' commitment to the organization. There are well-known and legitimate organizational paths to promotion and success in the organization.

- *Bureaucracy* is a more complex concept that encompasses all the terms mentioned above; in fact, a classic definition of bureaucracy is the extent to which an organization has all of the above properties; that is, a bureaucracy is an organizational structure characterized by hierarchy of authority; division of labor; impersonal decision making; formal rules, regulations, and procedures; and a career perspective.

Concepts that are complex and composed of other concepts, such as bureaucracy, are sometimes distinguished by the term *construct*, which implies a concept with multiple dimensions. This is a subtle distinction and one that we do not emphasize in this book; we continue to use *concept* and *construct* to refer to abstractions with specific definitions, regardless of complexity.

Alienation

Alienation is a complex sociological concept defined as the extent to which an individual rejects the common practices and conventions of a group, organization, or even society itself. At first blush, the concept may not seem that complex to you; you simply must specify what an individual is alienated from—the group, organization, or society. But, a review of the literature on alienation, especially the conceptual literature, suggests that there are multiple views or varieties of alienation. Consider the following concepts and their definitions:

- *Powerlessness* is the extent to which individuals believe that they cannot control the outcomes of their behavior.

- *Meaninglessness* is the degree to which individuals understand the events in which they are engaged; the individual is unclear on what he or she ought to believe.

- *Normlessness* is the sense in which an individual believes that socially unapproved behaviors are required to reach a certain goal.

- *Isolation* is the sense in which an individual believes that his or her valued goals are not highly valued by others in the group, organization, or society.

- *Self-estrangement* is the extent to which a person experiences himself or herself as alien; that is, individuals are at odds with themselves.

All five of these concepts are aspects of alienation. What becomes clear is that alienation is complex, with multiple variations. We have seen that alienation can be conceptualized as a construct with at least five varieties (Hoy, 1972; Seeman, 1959).

There is no substitute for a comprehensive review of the literature to get a good fix on the idea that you are interested in studying. Students often have a sense of what they want to explore, but to understand and conceptualize the idea, extensive review is imperative. For example, the construct of alienation, as we have seen, has a rich theoretical history. At the very minimum, you would want to consult the classic works of Marx, Durkheim, Weber, and Etzioni, as well as Seeman's synthesis.

School Climate

If you visit a dozen or so elementary schools, you will probably be struck by how different they seem. Some schools feel like prisons; others seem like efficient factories; and still others have a strong sense of community. What makes these schools feel different? Maybe it is the principals: Some are authoritarian and others are laid back. Perhaps it is the friendliness of the teachers that explains the variety. Something is just different about these elementary schools, and it does not take long to sense it. What would you call these different impressions of the school? *Character*, *atmosphere*, *culture*, *ideology*, *tone*, *identity*, and *school personality* or *school climate* are all terms you might use.

One challenge is to select the "right" set of concepts to describe the school environment. In other words, you need to conceptualize the "feel" of the school. Here again, it is important to examine the theoretical literature in order to find a useful framework to describe the idea that piques your curiosity. One might conceptualize school climate in half a dozen different ways, but I will select one perspective to illustrate the conceptualization of the atmosphere of the school. The concept of choice for me is school climate. What is school climate? How is climate defined? What are the critical aspects of school climate? You have heard the term bandied around, but if you are going to study school climate, a careful definition is an essential starting point.

We begin by viewing school climate as a multidimensional construct—that is, composed of a number of concepts. Consider the following definition:

- *School climate* is the "personality of the school," defined by the leadership of the principal and the interactions of the teachers.

Let's start with the leadership of the principal. The principal's behavior can be examined in terms of the following three kinds of interaction or leadership patterns:

1. *Supportive* principal behavior is action that reflects basic concern for teachers, help and respect for teachers, and general openness in interactions with teachers.

2. *Directive* principal behavior is rigid, close, controlling supervision of teachers.

3. *Restrictive* principal behavior hinders rather than facilitates teacher work; the principal burdens teachers with reports, meetings, and busywork.

Next, consider the interaction patterns of the teachers in terms of how they relate with each other. As with the principal-teacher interactions, the following are three major patterns of teacher-teacher interactions:

1. *Collegial* behavior is teacher behavior that is open, professional, accepting, and respectful: Teachers are proud of their school and respect the professional competence of their colleagues.

2. *Intimate* behavior reflects a cohesive and strong network of social support: Teachers know each other well, socialize with each other, and are good friends.

3. *Disengaged* behavior refers to a lack of meaning and focus in teacher professional work: Teachers are simply going through the motions and are not committed to teaching.

Note that the six previous concepts describe the school in terms of principal and teacher behavior. There is one more climate concept that evolves from this perspective—a more general property of the organization—the openness of the school climate.

An *open school climate* is one in which the principal's leadership is supportive, nondirective, and not restrictive. Teachers respond with a commitment to teaching and learning, close intimate social relations, and collegial relations among themselves. There is a genuine and authentic character to the open and transparent relationships in the professional activities of the school. This latter construct, school openness, is the most general and inclusive of the six earlier concepts.

To review, we started this discussion with the observation that schools give different initial impressions to observers; we sense the feel or tone of the school even in brief visits.

How do we "get a handle" on this feeling of schools? We considered a number of terms to describe the tone of the school and decided to view the atmosphere of the school from a climate perspective. We likened the school climate to the personality of an individual; that is, *climate is to organization what personality is to individual.* Then to illustrate further, we defined the basic elements of school climate: supportive, directive, restrictive principal behavior and collegial, intimate, and disengaged teacher behavior. Finally, we defined an open school climate in terms of these six school characteristics. The point of the exercise was to demonstrate the process of conceptualization and to identify some other concepts and constructs that we find useful as we proceed in this text. Clearly, this is not the only perspective to view school climate; in fact, others may be more useful to you depending on just what you want to study. Furthermore, a notion of school culture, for some purposes, may provide a better view of the school's personality. Good reviews of other perspectives on school climate and culture are found in the work of Hoy and his colleagues (Hoy & Miskel, 2008; Hoy & Sabo, 1998; Hoy, Tarter, & Kottkamp, 1991).

We now turn to three more organizational concepts and their definitions—trust, self-regulatory climate, and academic optimism.

Trust

Trust is a little like air—you don't think about it until it is scarce or absent (Baier, 1986). Trust is fundamental to the effective functioning of all social systems, including schools and society itself; it is viewed as the "lubricant," greasing the way for efficient operation when participants have confidence in the words and deeds of their colleagues and their leaders (Arrow, 1974).

We propose the following general definition of trust based on an extensive review of the literature (Tschannen-Moran & Hoy, 2000), and then move to trust in organizations, particularly the trust of the school faculty.

- *Trust* is an individual's or a group's willingness to be vulnerable to another party based on the confidence that the party is benevolent, reliable, competent, honest, and open.

This construct is complex and calls for the definition of another half a dozen concepts (Hoy & Tschannen-Moran, 1999):

- *Vulnerability* is the willingness to put oneself or one's group at risk by trusting another individual or group.

- *Benevolence* is the confidence that one's well-being or something one cares about will be protected by the trusted individual or group.

- *Reliability* is the extent to which one can count on another individual or group to come through with what is needed.

- *Competence* is the knowledge or skill level on which the individual or group depends.

- *Honesty* is the character, integrity, and authenticity of the individual or group.

- *Openness* is the extent to which relevant information is not withheld from those making themselves vulnerable.

Just like most of the concepts we have examined thus far, you can see that the construct of trust is complex with a number of aspects: Trust is vulnerability, benevolence, reliability, competence, honesty, and openness. That is, there are six concepts that constitute our working definition of trust. Are you interested in any particular aspect of trust or all the elements? What begins as a rather simple inquiry into the notion of trust quickly evolves into a set of multiple questions and concepts that need your attention and answers. Furthermore, as a student of schools, you may be interested in the collective trust of schools, that is, *faculty trust in the principal, faculty trust in colleagues*, or *faculty trust in students and parents*. Perhaps you are more intrigued with *parent trust* in the school, principal, or teachers. Obviously, trust has many referents. The researcher needs to decide the focus and refine the concept. Clearly, a good working definition and conceptualization of trust is critical, which again typically comes from a systematic study of the research. There is no substitute for a careful reading of the literature; relevant theory is a virtual gold mine for concepts of all kinds.

Self-Regulated Climate

Self-regulation is a key to success, whether it is in solving complex problems or behaving appropriately in difficult situations. Self-regulated individuals act on their own volition and possess the inner agency to control their efforts (Reeve, Ryan, Deci, & Jang, 2008). A self-regulatory climate, however, is neither an individual state nor the sum of individual regulatory beliefs or behaviors; instead, it is a social feature of a school built through cooperative, trustworthy, and academic student-teacher interactions.

Self-regulatory climate has its roots in Deci and Ryan's self-determination theory (Deci & Ryan, 1985, 2008). The emphasis placed on self reflects the inherent motivation of individuals to learn and develop, whereas the emphasis placed on climate reflects a normative disposition of schools that nurture student capacity (Adams, Forsyth, Dollarhide, Miskell, & Ware, 2015). Adams and his colleagues postulate that a self-regulatory school is structured to provide three basic supports for student psychological needs: autonomy, competence, and relatedness.

- *Autonomy-support* is a set of cooperative and trustworthy interactions between teachers and students that enable the creation of a student-centered environment.

- *Competence-support* reinforces high academic expectations, achievable goals, and academic excellence.

- *Relatedness-support* promotes positive interactions between students and teachers.

These three conditions are interrelated, interactive, and form a climate of self-regulation. In brief, self-regulatory climate is an environment that supports and reinforces the psychological needs of autonomy, competence, and relatedness in students (Adams, Forsyth, Ware, Dollarhide, Miskell, 2015). Like the previous constructs in this chapter, self-regulatory climate is complex and is composed of three interrelated concepts.

Academic Optimism

The academic optimism of the school is the last concept we briefly consider in this chapter. One of the challenges facing students of schools is to find organizational properties of schools that make a difference in the achievement of students. This task is complicated by the fact that the socioeconomic level of the school is such a powerful shaper of student performance that it overwhelms the association between other school properties and achievement; in fact, the influence of most school properties on achievement vanishes once the influence on social factors has been controlled (Hoy, Tarter, & Woolfolk Hoy, 2006b). One of the few exceptions to this finding is the concept of academic optimism, but to understand the construct, it is necessary to define three other concepts:

1. *Academic emphasis* is the extent to which a school faculty is driven by a quest for academic excellence and achievement.

2. *Collective efficacy* is the perceived collective judgment of teachers as a whole that they can organize and execute the actions required to have positive effects on students.

3. *Faculty trust in parents and students* is a collective school property that describes the extent to which the faculty is willing to make itself vulnerable to parents and students based on the confidence that these parties are benevolent, reliable, competent, honest, and open.

Optimism is an overarching construct that unites efficacy, trust, and academic emphasis because each concept contains a sense of the possible. Efficacy means that the faculty believes in itself; the faculty can make a positive difference. Trust reflects the belief that parents, teachers, and students can cooperate to improve learning; the faculty believes in its students. Finally, academic emphasis is enacted behavior prompted by these trust and efficacy beliefs. Thus, the following construct is proposed:

- *Academic optimism* is the collective belief of the faculty that it can make a difference, that students can learn, and that high academic performance can be achieved (Hoy et al., 2006a, 2006b).

For the present, we have a rich set of concepts to draw on as we proceed in this chapter. Throughout the book, we use these concepts as well as others that we develop as needed. You should understand that concepts and constructs are abstract terms with specific definitions. There are several kinds of definitions. Thus far, all our examples are theoretical, that is, conceptual and **constitutive definitions**. Why do we use three different terms to refer to the same thing? The answer is simple—because as you read other sources, different authors have their own preferences. For example, Kerlinger (1986) uses constitutive definition rather than either theoretical or **conceptual definition**. It does not matter: All three designations have the same meaning— *definitions that explain the construct by using other concepts and words to make the meaning clear and easy to understand.*

VARIABLES

What is a *variable*? All of us use the term as we talk to other students and professors about research. Can you give a clear definition of a variable? It may be easier said than done. First, variables are related to concepts. All the concepts that we developed thus far can be transformed to variables. Constructs and concepts become variables when we define them in terms of a set of operations that measure them, that is, when we provide operational definitions to match their constitutive ones. Of course, the operational definitions must capture the true meaning of the constructs (i.e., be a **valid measure)**, and they must provide a consistent and objective measurement (i.e., be reliable).

Before we offer a definition of a variable, there are three general terms you must be clear about: (1) *research objects*, (2) *properties of the objects*, and (3) *values of properties* (Charters, 1992). Objects *are the persons, places, or things on which you conduct your research*; the object is also called the **unit of analysis**. Usually, the objects of a study in educational research are people or persons (students, teachers, administrators, school board members), but they can be places, such as schools or day care centers, or they can be things, such as school newspaper editorials, bond elections, or curriculum programs.

Properties *are the characteristics or attributes of an object.* Consider the size of a dress, the height or weight of a student, or the length of a school day or school year. Clearly, properties are not the same as the objects; rather, properties describe some characteristic of the object in terms of size, color, shape, or temperature, to give just a few examples. There are many properties that we can use to describe things, and these attributes help us understand important differences and similarities among objects.

A variable *is a property that takes on different values as circumstances and situations change*; the value *is a number that represents either the magnitude of the variable* (e.g., an individual's height), *or a category of the variable* (e.g., male or female). Height can be measured in inches, and the larger the number, the greater the height. On the other hand, gender is measured in terms of the categories of male (1) and female (2). Both height and gender are variables, but for height the number represents magnitude, whereas for gender the value represents a category. Variables must have at least two categories of measure; if they have only one category of measure, they are constants, not variables. Two other important facts—the values for variables must be exhaustive and mutually exclusive. *Exhaustive* means that each object can be assigned a value, and *mutually exclusive* means that each object can have one and only one value.

Let's consider a few examples of properties (variables) of teachers (objects), some of which are variables of magnitude (continuous or degree of variation) and others are variables of category.

> *Height* (magnitude: continuous or degree of variation—higher means taller)
>
> *Teaching level* (categorical: elementary, middle, or high school)
>
> *Self-concept* (magnitude: continuous—higher means stronger)
>
> *Political party* (categorical: Republican, Democrat, Independent, other)
>
> *Teaching experience* (magnitude: continuous—higher means longer)
>
> *Level of expertise* (categorical: neophyte, advanced, master)

The list could be extended at will, but the point is that these are variables that we might use to study teachers. We could develop another list of variables for principals, superintendents, or schools; in fact, most of the concepts developed in the previous section were characteristics of schools, that is, school variables.

Kinds of Variables

There are a number of ways to classify variables. Our treatment here is to identify several of the more important and useful distinctions. We begin by classifying variables by type of variation.

CATEGORICAL AND CONTINUOUS VARIABLES. We already alluded to this distinction in the list of variables above. *When the variations of the variable are associated with specific categories, we refer to them as* **categorical variables**. Charters (1992) calls these **in-kind variables** because the variation represents different kinds of categories. Such variables usually do not fall along any continuum of measurement; in fact, the variation is simply a matter of identifying a property as having two or more distinct categories—for example, sick or healthy. The following are a few illustrations of categorical variables, in particular variations in kind, followed by a specification of the categories.

> *Leadership style:* statesman, task-oriented, social, passive
>
> *Career orientation:* place bound, career bound
>
> *Mobility pattern:* upwardly mobile, ambivalent, indifferent
>
> *Locus of control:* internal, external
>
> *Learning style:* visual, verbal

Remember, there must be at least two distinct categories. The name of the variable does not necessarily give you a clue to the kind of variable. When dealing with a categorical variable, the categories and the implicated values should be clearly stated.

Variables that vary by magnitude along an ordered continuum are called **continuous variables**. The numbers or values indicate the magnitude of the variable, specifically the value represents how far along a given dimension the actual object lies; the larger the number, the further out on the dimension. The numbers are not merely names for categories. Continuous variables are also called **in-degree variables** (Charters, 1992) because the number is a quantitative measure of degree. The name of the property often provides a clue: level, length, index, quotient, and size, height—all suggest a quantitative measure such that the property varies in degree along a given continuum. Consider a few illustrations:

> *Age:* the larger the number, the older the individual
>
> *Class size:* the larger the number, the larger the class

Salary: the larger the number, the higher the salary

IQ: the larger the number, the more intelligent

Experience: the larger the number, the more experienced

All the above variables suggest continuous measurement from low to high. However, sometimes the name is misleading. For example, we assume that age is a continuous variable, and theoretically it is, but some researchers measure it as a categorical variable by grouping respondents into three categories—young, middle-aged, and mature. Why? Although respondents may be reluctant to give their exact age on a questionnaire, they may be willing to place themselves into one of a few broad and clearly defined categories. Some people are vain, and others are suspicious that the research may try to identify them and their responses. The only way to be certain of the kind of variable is to examine its operational measure.

INDEPENDENT AND DEPENDENT VARIABLES. Another way, perhaps the most common way to classify a variable is in terms of its function. An independent variable *is the presumed causal variable in a relationship*, and the **dependent variable** *is the presumed effect variable* (Kerlinger, 1986). The key word in these definitions is *presumed*, because in social and behavioral research we can never be sure that a given variable causes another to change. We presume or theorize that it does, but we cannot be certain. We predict from the independent to the dependent variable: The independent is the antecedent, and the dependent is the consequent. In the statement "If x, then y," x is the independent variable and y is the dependent variable. A similar convention exists in mathematics: The x variable is the independent variable, and the y variable is the dependent variable—for example, when you graph a function.

Consider this statement from psychology: "Frustration (x) leads to aggression (y)." The presumed cause is frustration, and the presumed consequence is aggression; thus, frustration is the independent variable and aggression is the dependent variable. In some relations, it is clear which variable is the independent variable, but in others it is not. In examining the relation between experience and pupil-control orientation, the independent variable is clearly experience because pupil-control orientation cannot cause any variation in experience. Similarly, in a study of intelligence and achievement, it is more likely that intelligence influences achievement rather than the other way around. There are many relationships in the social and behavioral sciences, however, in which the causation flows both ways; that is, the independent variable affects the dependent variable, but then the dependent variable influences the independent variable. This is an example of **reciprocal causation** because the casual connection flows both ways. For example, the personal characteristics of an individual influence behavior, but behavior in turn influences personal attributes, a case of reciprocal causation. The distinction between independent and dependent variables is useful if not always exact.

MEASURED AND MANIPULATED VARIABLES. All the variables that we provided and illustrated thus far are **measured variables**—*variables that are defined by operations that are measured.* We use some tool to measure the value of the variable—a scale for weight, a test for achievement, or a questionnaire for more abstract properties. Measured variables are straightforward. Find the right tool and measure them.

A **manipulated variable** *is a variable that has been directly controlled by the researcher in an experiment.* Consider the concept of leadership. A measured variable of leadership is the score on a descriptive questionnaire where subordinates describe leader behavior. Note that the behavior has already happened.

A manipulated variable of leadership is one that is controlled by the researcher. For example, a study may be designed in which the researcher hires actors to play different roles for various groups. In one group, the leader behaves according to an autocratic script; in another group, the leader follows a democratic script; and in the third group, the leader maintains no control or influence in the group. In the design of this experiment, leadership is manipulated and defined as autocratic, democratic, or laissez-faire—three leadership styles (Lewin, Lippitt, & White, 1939). In this case, the variable is a manipulated categorical variable. Manipulated variables are categorical because they are the manipulations of groups in an experiment. For example, in the experiment with three leadership styles, there is *only one variable*, leadership style, with three categories or variations—autocratic, democratic, or laissez faire. Thus, we have illustrated the difference between a measured and a manipulated variable.

In sum, manipulated variables are the exclusive domain of experimental research. Measured variables are the properties of objects in both experimental and nonexperimental research. Virtually all the variables in nonexperimental research are measured; however, in experimental research, only the dependent variable is measured. In other words, the independent variable is manipulated and its effect measured in the dependent variable. In the end, what researchers are trying to do is to explain the variability, or **variance**, in the dependent variable by manipulating some independent variable or set of independent variables.

MEDIATING AND MODERATING VARIABLES. One other distinction in types of variables should be briefly addressed—mediator versus moderator variables. A **moderating variable** is one that affects the direction and/or strength of the relation between an independent and a dependent variable. That is, in a correlational analysis framework, a moderator changes the basic relation between the independent and dependent variables. For example, in Fielder's leadership theory, he demonstrates that the "favorableness of the group setting" moderates the relationship between leadership and effectiveness. When the group situation is only favorable, then there is a **positive correlation** between a human relations style of leadership and group effectiveness, but when the situation is either very favorable or very unfavorable, then there is a negative relation between human relations leadership and effectiveness (Fiedler, 1967).

In contrast, a **mediating variable** (sometimes called an **intervening variable**) explains the relationship between the independent and dependent variables; it does not change the relation, it explains it. For example, the presence of a teacher aide enhances student achievement; that is, having a teacher aide is positively related to higher student achievement. Why? How? What explains the relationship between having an aide and increased student achievement? The degree of individual attention explains the relation between having a teacher aide and student achievement; hence, degree of individual attention is a mediating variable between the two variables.

In sum, a moderating variable influences the strength of a relation between two other variables, whereas a mediating variable explains the relation between those variables. For example, consider the relation between socioeconomic status (SES) and frequency of breast self-exams (BSE). Age might be a moderating variable because the relation is likely strong for older women and less strong or nonexistent for younger women. Education, however, might be a mediating variable that explains why there is a relation between SES and BSE. Remove the effect of education, and the relation between SES and BSE disappears (Baron & Kenny, 1986). There are other useful distinctions in variables, but we can stop here and add when appropriate.

OPERATIONALIZING CONCEPTS

We now turn to transforming concepts and constructs into variables. Researchers cannot do quantitative empirical research without converting their concepts into variables. **Theoretical definitions** are not sufficient; operational definitions are required. We must change our ideas into concepts and our concepts into variables. An operational definition *explicates the variable as a set of specific operations that are measured or manipulated.*

In the previous section, we gave many examples of variables that were relatively easy to measure—for example, age, experience, gender, height, weight, political party, and school level. Let's look at some operational measures for more abstract concepts, those defined theoretically in the beginning of this chapter. Although every one of these terms can be measured (operationalized), we illustrate only a few. A good exercise for you: Find operational definitions for some of the other referenced concepts.

In education, scales are measured using pencil and paper questionnaires to operationalize many of our concepts. Let's begin with school climate. There are a number of different ways to measure school climate (e.g., see www.waynekhoy.com), but we will illustrate using the Organizational Climate Description Questionnaire-RE (OCDQ-RE), a questionnaire designed to tap the climate of elementary schools. The OCDQ-RE is a 42-item questionnaire that is administered to the teachers of a school. The items are then grouped into subgroups that define the six elements of school climate—supportive, directive, and restrictive principal behavior and collegial, intimate, and disengaged behavior. The first three concepts define the leader behavior of the principal (principal-teacher interactions), and the last three describe the teacher-teacher interactions. Once all six elements of climate are measured, then it is possible to determine the extent to which the school climate is open or closed.

Consider the concept of supportive principal behavior. First, we provide the theoretical definition of the concept and then the operational measure of the variable.

- *Concept* (theoretical definition)*: Supportive principal behavior is action that reflects basic concern for teachers, help and respect for teachers, and a general openness and support in interactions with teachers.*

- *Variable* (operational definition): *Supportive principal behavior is operationalized by the following set of items from the OCDQ-RE.*

DIRECTIONS: Please indicate the extent to which each statement describes your school.

1 = Rarely OCCURS; 2 = Sometimes OCCURS; 3 = Often OCCURS; 4 = Frequently OCCURS

The principal goes out of his/her way to help teachers... 1 2 3 4

The principal uses constructive criticism.. 1 2 3 4

The principal explains his/her reasons for criticism to teachers............................ 1 2 3 4

The principal listens to and accepts teachers' suggestions..................................... 1 2 3 4

The principal looks out for the personal welfare of the teachers...........................1 2 3 4

The principal treats teachers as equals...1 2 3 4

The principal compliments teachers...1 2 3 4

The principal is easy to understand...1 2 3 4

The principal goes out of his/her way to show appreciation to teachers..............1 2 3 4

Now look at a definition of another dimension of elementary school climate.

- *Concept* (theoretical definition): *Collegial teacher behavior is behavior that is open, professional, accepting, and respectful; teachers are proud of their school and respect the professional competence of their colleagues.*

- *Variable* (operational definition): *Collegial teacher behavior is operationalized by the following set of items from the OCDQ-RE.*

DIRECTIONS: Please indicate the extent to which each statement describes your school.

1 = Rarely OCCURS; 2 = Sometimes OCCURS; 3 = Often OCCURS; 4 = Frequently OCCURS

Teachers accomplish their work with vim, vigor, and pleasure....................................1 2 3 4

*Teachers leave school immediately after school is over..1 2 3 4

Most teachers here accept the faults of their colleagues..1 2 3 4

Teachers help and support each other..1 2 3 4

Teachers are proud of their school...1 2 3 4

*Teachers socialize together in small, select groups..1 2 3 4

Teachers respect the professional competence of their colleagues.............................1 2 3 4

*Scored in reverse

As you know from our earlier discussion of school climate, there are four other aspects, each with an operational definition. In actual research, teachers in the school respond to the items, the items are scored, and then each individual dimension score is averaged to obtain the school score on that aspect of climate. The items of the OCDQ are called

4-point **Likert items**, items that indicate the degree to which the respondent agrees with the statement or the extent to which it occurs. Although the climate measure is composed of 4-point Likert items, Likert items can have 5-, 6-, or 7-point responses. To get a more complete understanding of these operational variables, go to www.waynekhoy.com and administer one of the climate measures to your school and score it according to the directions supplied.

Let's review. We use the term *theoretical definition* to refer to a conceptual definition; the concept is defined in terms of words. But, the concept must be transformed into a variable to conduct research. For example, supportive principal behavior is operationalized as a set of Likert items where the teacher describes the extent to which principal behaviors occur: *rarely occurs, sometimes occurs, often occurs,* and *very frequently occurs.* The items are summed to get an individual score on each dimension (supportive, directive, and restrictive principal behavior and collegial, intimate, disengaged teacher behavior), and then the scores for each dimension are averaged to get a school score on the variables; the higher the score, the more of the property or characteristic of the variable. In the case of the OCDQ-RE, an *openness index* is *calculated by combining all the dimensional scores on the instrument to indicate the extent to which the school climate is open.* One final point: All the variables measured by the OCDQ-RE have been tested and refined to demonstrate that the variables are reliable and valid: They measure consistently what they are supposed to measure. In fact, all the variables that we describe in this chapter are valid and reliable.

Of course, not all concepts are operationalized by a set of Likert items. For example, consider hierarchy of authority.

- *Concept* (theoretical definition): *Hierarchy of authority is the extent to which a position is under the control and supervision of a higher office.*

- *Variable* (operational definition): *Hierarchy of authority is the number of supervisory levels in the chain of command.*

Note the difference between the theoretical definition and the operational one. The distinction demonstrates the conversion of a concept to a variable. This particular operational definition is direct, objective, and relatively easy to apply to most school organizations.

We end this section on operationalizing concepts by examining the concepts of academic emphasis, collective efficacy, and faculty trust in teachers and parents.

- *Concept* (theoretical definition): *Academic emphasis is the extent to which a school faculty is driven by a quest for high academic excellence and achievement.*

- *Variable* (operational definition): *Academic emphasis is operationalized by the following set of items (see www.waynekhoy.com).*

DIRECTIONS: Please indicate the extent to which each statement describes your school.

1 = Rarely OCCURS; 2 = Sometimes OCCURS; 3 = Often OCCURS; 4 = Frequently OCCURS

The school sets high standards for academic success... 1 2 3 4

Students respect others who get good grades... 1 2 3 4

Students in this school can achieve the goals that are set for them...................... 1 2 3 4

Students seek extra work so they can get good grades.. 1 2 3 4

Students try hard to improve on previous work... 1 2 3 4

Teachers in this school believe that their students
have the ability to achieve academically.. 1 2 3 4

Academic achievement is recognized and acknowledged by the school.............. 1 2 3 4

The learning environment is orderly and serious.. 1 2 3 4

- *Concept* (theoretical definition)*: Collective efficacy is the perceived collective judgment that teachers as a whole can organize and execute the actions required to have positive effects on students.*

- *Variable* (operational definition) *Collective efficacy is operationalized by the following set of items (see www.waynekhoy.com).*

DIRECTIONS: Please indicate the extent to which each statement is true of your school along a continuum from Strongly Disagree (1) to Strongly Agree (6).

Teachers in this school are able to get
through to the most difficult students... 1 2 3 4 5 6

Teachers here are confident they
will be able to motivate their students.. 1 2 3 4 5 6

*If a child doesn't want to
learn teachers here give up... 1 2 3 4 5 6

*Teachers here don't have the
skills needed to produce meaningful learning.. 1 2 3 4 5 6

Teachers in this school believe
that every child can learn... 1 2 3 4 5 6

These students come to school ready to learn....................................... 1 2 3 4 5 6

Home life provides so many advantages
that students here are bound to learn.. 1 2 3 4 5 6

*Students here just aren't motivated to learn...................................... 1 2 3 4 5 6

*Teachers in this school do not have the
skills to deal with student disciplinary problems.............................. 1 2 3 4 5 6

The opportunities in this community help
ensure that these students will learn... 1 2 3 4 5 6

*Learning is more difficult at this school
because students are worried about their safety................................. 1 2 3 4 5 6

*Drug and alcohol abuse in the community
make learning difficult for students here.. 1 2 3 4 5 6

*Scored in reverse.

- *Concept* (theoretical definition): *Faculty trust in parents and students is the school faculty's willingness to be vulnerable to parents and students based on the confidence that they are benevolent, reliable, competent, honest, and open.*

- *Variable* (operational definition): *Faculty trust in parents and teachers is operationalized by the following set of items (see www. waynekhoy.com).*

DIRECTIONS: Please indicate the extent to which each statement is true of your school along a continuum from Strongly Disagree (1) to Strongly Agree (6).

Teachers in this school trust their students.. 1 2 3 4 5 6

Teachers in this school trust the parents.. 1 2 3 4 5 6

Students in this school care about each other..................................... 1 2 3 4 5 6

Parents in this school are reliable in their commitments.................. 1 2 3 4 5 6

Students in this school can be counted on to do their work............. 1 2 3 4 5 6

Teachers can count on parental support.. 1 2 3 4 5 6

Teachers here believe that students are competent learners.............................1 2 3 4 5 6

Teachers think that most of the parents do a good job.....................................1 2 3 4 5 6

Teachers can believe what parents tell them...1 2 3 4 5 6

*Students here are secretive...1 2 3 4 5 6

*Scored in reverse

Finally, consider the following construct:

- *Concept* (theoretical definition): *Academic optimism is the collective belief of the faculty that it can make a difference, that students can learn, and that high academic performance can be achieved.*

- *Variable* (operational definition): *Academic optimism is operationalized by combining the scores of academic emphasis, collective efficacy, and faculty trust in parents and students.*

RESEARCH PROBLEMS

Insomnia is a frequent problem among older citizens. In common parlance, a problem is a difficulty that causes discomfort or worry. This general definition conveys the nature of a problem, but it is insufficient for scientific purposes. We need a more specific delineation that suggests how researchers can address the issue. In science, a research problem *is a query about the relationship between two or more variables*. It foreshadows the research and is an important element of any research proposal (see "Elements of a Proposal," Appendix A). Note that the statement of the problem is a question in need of an answer.

Let's consider a few research problems from psychology and teaching:

1. Does massive reinforcement improve reading achievement?

2. Does teacher optimism promote student optimism?

3. Does student optimism lead to higher levels of classroom performance?

4. Does self-regulatory climate foster autonomous student motivation?

Here are a few more complicated research problems:

4. Under what conditions do specific goals improve mathematics achievement?

5. Under what conditions does student frustration lead to aggression?

All these are possible research problems because they all are questions; they inquire about the relation between two variables; and the questions all lend themselves to empirical testing. In other words, a good research problem meets three criteria:

1. The problem is a question.

2. The question is about the relation among variables.

3. The relationship is capable of empirical testing.

Now let's develop some research questions with the concepts we examined in this chapter. Consider the following:

1. Is bureaucratic structure in schools related to teacher alienation?

2. Is organizational climate related to teacher alienation?

Both these meet the general criteria of a research problem: They are questions about the relationships between variables, and the questions seem capable of empirical testing. But, both are general questions that could be developed and specified. For example, what is there about bureaucratic structure that may promote alienation? Furthermore, what kind of alienation would it produce? What aspect of bureaucracy is the culprit? We could narrow and specify the question by asking, "Does hierarchy of authority promote a sense of powerlessness among teachers?" Furthermore, if we are familiar with the conceptualizations of structure and alienation that we outlined earlier, we could develop a rather extensive set of questions, about 25 research questions or so: for example, "Is hierarchy of authority related to meaninglessness, to normlessness, to isolation, and to self-estrangement?" We could generate a similar list of questions about division of labor, impersonality, formalization, and career orientation. As the researcher grapples with these questions and tries to formulate answers, the analysis inevitably undergoes change and refinement. We ask ourselves what elements of structure promote alienation and what kind of alienation? What elements of structure are unrelated to alienation? Which particular kinds of alienation? What is more important in creating alienation—the *amount* or the *kind of structure?* In sum, the general question about structure and alienation leads to a host of more specific questions about the relationships among the elements of each construct.

The second research problem about school climate and alienation also has many possibilities. These are rich constructs with much potential. See how many specific research problems you can generate from this second general question. Are these questions worth answering? Why? The process of generating fascinating research questions depends on a number of factors, including your imagination, your knowledge, and your scholarship. There is no substitute for a rigorous review of the literature (see Appendix A) as you try to formulate and conceptualize your research problem. Build on the work of other theorists and scholars—stand on their shoulders. Read, read, and read. Once you get some rich conceptual frameworks, you will find it easy and enjoyable to create interesting research questions. Given the conceptualizations of just a few constructs at the beginning of this chapter, consider what you can do with the following general questions:

1. Is there a relationship between hierarchy of authority and supportive administrative behavior?

2. Is there a relationship between formalization and sense of powerlessness?

3. Is there a relationship between collegial teacher behavior and faculty trust?

4. Is there a relationship between academic optimism and faculty trust?

5. Is there a relationship between self-regulatory climate and student achievement?

6. Is there a relationship between bureaucratic structure and academic optimism?

How many more general queries can you generate with these concepts? Furthermore, these general questions suggest a myriad of other related and more specific issues. What is the object of your analysis? Teachers? Students? Administrators? The list of possibilities goes on. We have just begun. Add the concept of school achievement, and the possibilities escalate. Add student self-concept, and the options continue to mount, and on and on. Build conceptual capital as you take classes in education, administration, psychology, and sociology. Keep a concept notebook to record fascinating constructs and their meanings. Fill your mind as well as your notebook with concepts. Then as you begin to ask questions about their relationships, you will be amazed by the research possibilities.

Students ask, "How do I find good research questions?" Our answer is, "Observe, read, and take notes." Look for patterns of behavior and try to explain them. Search for fascinating constructs and theoretical perspectives. Use abstractions to shape your questions and answers. Read theoretically rich articles. Collect ideas and concepts, and ask how the ideas and concepts apply to schools. Good theory generates good research. So don't avoid the theoretical; embrace it, and apply it to the problems of practice. The application of theory to practice involves some practice itself, but it is a skill that can be learned and a habit to be cultivated. It may take you a while to figure out how to use the ideas of theory to develop important research questions, but the effort is worth the reward. A major purpose of this text is to help you along this journey of discovery.

SUMMARY

To understand research, it is imperative to comprehend the nature of concepts, constructs, variables, and research problems.

- *Concepts*, *constructs*, and *variables* are terms that are often used interchangeably, yet there are some subtle differences among them.

- Concepts are general abstractions that have specific definitions.

- Constructs are concepts, but they typically are more complex ones with multiple dimensions.

- Concepts and constructs are the stuff of theory; they are abstractions that are used to explain relations and general patterns of behavior.

- Variables are concepts that have operational measures.

- Variables are the properties of the object being studied; they are symbols that take on at least two numerical values.

- For some variables, the value represents a category, such as male or female, but for other variables like weight, the number represents the magnitude or degree of the variable along a continuum.

- There are many kinds of variables, but the most common distinction is between independent variables (the presumed causes) and dependent variables (the presumed effects).

- A research problem is a question about the relation of two or more variables, which frames a quantitative study.

- Ultimately, the researcher's challenge is to explain what causes the dependent variable to change (see "Elements of a Proposal," Appendix A).

1. What is the difference between a concept and a construct? Give a specific example of each. Define each in words. Can you define them as a set of operations?

2. Make up an operational definition for each of the following terms:

    A. reinforcement

    B. reading ability

    C. underachievement

    D. classroom management

    E. self-regulatory climate

    F. enabling structure

    G. classroom climate

3. Provide an example of a concept that can be measured either as a categorical variable or as a continuous variable. How many categories does the variable have, and what are they?

4. Define teaching style first as a categorical variable and then as a continuous variable. Next, define teaching style as an experimental variable and then as a measured variable.

5. What is the difference between a mediating and a moderating variable? Give an example of each.

6. Below are research problems from education. Study them and then construct a hypothesis for each.

    A. Does teacher feedback provide improvement in student performance?

    B. Does the openness of school climate influence student achievement?

    C. Do administrator beliefs about learning influence teacher performance?

    D. Under what conditions is direct teaching more effective than indirect teaching?

    E. Does socioeconomic status of students influence attitudes toward school?

    F. Is self-regulatory school climate related to school achievement?

7. Discuss the possibility of testing each of the following hypotheses.

    A. Collegial supervisors evaluate teachers more positively than do directive supervisors.

    B. Teachers with high **self-efficacy** have students with higher self-efficacy than teachers with low self-efficacy.

    C. The greater the cohesiveness of a faculty, the greater the faculty influence on teachers.

    D. Role conflict among teachers is a function of the extent of hierarchy in the school.

KEY TERMS

Academic emphasis (p. 27)

Academic optimism (p. 25)

Categorical variable (p. 30)

Collective efficacy (p. 27)

Conceptual definition (p. 28)

Constitutive definition (p. 28)

Continuous variable (p. 30)

Dependent variable (p. 31)

Faculty trust in parents
  and students (p. 27)

In-degree variable (p. 30)

In-kind variable (p. 30)

Intervening variable (p. 33)

Likert items (p. 36)

Manipulated variable (p. 32)

Measured variable (p. 32)

Mediating variable (p. 33)

Moderating variable (p. 33)

Positive correlation (p. 33)

Reciprocal causation (p. 32)

Self-efficacy (p. 43)

Self-regulatory climate (p. 26)

Theoretical definition (p. 33)

Unit of analysis (p. 28)

Valid measure (p. 28)

Variance (p. 32)

3

CONCEPTUAL FOUNDATIONS OF STATISTICS

In this chapter, we examine the conceptual foundations of statistics. The goal is to give you an appreciation and conceptual understanding of some basic statistical tests used in educational research. As we suggested in the first chapter, statistics are tools that empirical researchers use for analysis of quantitative research. Statistical tools are useful means and not ends in themselves. We focus on conceptual understanding and not on the technical details of computing the statistics, which is most often done in statistical courses or by using statistical packages, such as SPSS (Statistical Package for the Social Sciences) or SAS (Statistical Analysis System). We begin with a review of some basic descriptive statistics and then move to the conceptual underpinnings of inferential statistics, which are used to test **research hypotheses**. Read the text with a pencil in hand; check the simple calculations.

MEASURES OF CENTRAL TENDENCIES

There are three common measures of central tendency: **mean**, **mode**, and **median**. The mean is the most widely known statistic; it is the average of a set of numbers or scores. Most students compute their average test scores in a course without difficulty, and they understand what it means or represents—it is their typical test score. *The arithmetic average of some set of numbers in statistics is called the mean.* Summing all the scores in the set and then dividing the sum by the number of scores is the calculation of the mean. Consider the set of numbers (1, 2, 2, 3, 4, 6). The mean is calculated as follows:

Mean = Sum of the scores (Σ (scores)) divided by N (number of scores)

or

$$\text{Mean} = \frac{\sum (\text{scores})}{N}$$

Mean = $(1 + 2 + 2 + 3 + 4 + 6)/6 = 18/6 = 3$.

The mean or average of the set is 3, which represents a typical score for this set of data points. If the scores are reasonably consistent—that is, they don't vary wildly—then the mean is a good indication of the central tendency. If there are a few extreme scores, however, the mean can be distorted. Consider the set of numbers (1, 1, 1, 7, 1, 7). In this case, the mean is still 3, but it is not really typical. A few large and extreme numbers can distort the mean, and therein lies the possible rub of using the mean to describe a set of scores as typical. For example, in the previous set of numbers (1, 1, 1, 7, 1, 7), 1 is clearly more typical than 3.

The mode is the most frequent number in a set of scores. In the above set (1, 1, 1, 7, 1, 7), the mode is 1, the most frequent number in the distribution, and in this case, it is a good standard to describe the typical score of this set of numbers. But again, just as with the mean, the mode can be misleading. For example, suppose you give a test to 30 students and most students score close to 88; in fact, when you compute the mean you get 88. Yet there were five people who got 100 and only three who actually scored 88. Which is the better measure of central tendency, the mean (88) or the mode (100)? Clearly, the mean is more typical of the distribution of scores.

The median is the middle score of a distribution of numbers. To compute the median, do the following:

1. *Rank the numbers* or scores from low to high.

2. *Find the middle* number or score:

   - If there is an odd number of scores, for example, 11 numbers in the set, simply add 1 to the total number and divide by 2; the resulting number represents how far to go to find the median. Consider the numbers in the set (1, 2, 2, 2, 3, 5, 6, 7, 7, 8, 12). Since the set has 11 numbers (an odd number), add 1 to 11 and divide by 2: 12/2 = 6. The sixth number in the set is 5, and it is the median or middle score.

   - But, if there is an even number of scores, simply average the two middle scores. For example, consider the set (1, 2, 2, 2, 4, 5, 6, 7, 7, 8), which has 10 scores in the distribution. You simply add the fifth and sixth scores and divide by 2; hence, in this example the median is (4 + 5)/2 = 4.5. The median is the middle score, which is 4.5 in this case.

The median is the middle score in the distribution of ranked numbers; it is the point at which half the numbers are larger and half are smaller. When there are a few very high or very low scores, however, the median or mode may represent better the central tendency than does the mean.

In sum, the mean, mode, and median are the three most common measures of central tendency; they are indicators of how typical a given score is in a distribution of numbers, but none of these indicators gives you a sense of how the scores are distributed, that is, how much variability there is in the set of numbers.

MEASURES OF VARIABILITY

Let's now turn our attention to how much variability there is in a set of numbers. How are the scores distributed? How much do they vary? We consider three measures of variability: the **range**, the average deviation, and the **standard deviation** (*SD*).

The range is the difference between the highest and lowest scores in a set of numbers, but it is also given as the span of scores beginning with the lowest score and ending with the highest score, as in the range of 89 to 144 (or, alternately, the range is 55). The range is direct and simple, but a little crude because it only describes in broad strokes the limits of the scores; it does not tell us what is happening in between the extremes.

The average deviation from the mean is just what the phrase suggests: We find the mean, then find the deviation from the mean for each number (subtract the mean from the number), and then average all the deviations to get a typical departure of the scores from the mean. Conceptually, that makes sense, but unfortunately, we always get the same average deviation because half the scores will deviate above the mean and the other half below the mean; consequently, when you add the deviations you always get 0. Thus, the average deviation is always 0 and not useful. Take an example. Consider the set of numbers (1, 2, 3, 4, 5, 3, 3). The mean is 21/7 = 3. The deviations from the mean are −2, −1, 0, 1, 2, 0, and 0, respectively, and the sum is therefore 0. Zero divided by 7 is 0. Zero is always the average deviation from the mean because half the scores are above the mean and the other half are the same amount below the mean, and 0 divided by any number is 0. Try it yourself with a small set of numbers. Why bother with the average deviation from the mean? Only to help you understand the concept of a standard deviation from the mean.

The standard deviation *from the mean is the extent to which scores vary from the mean—the typical deviation from the mean for a set of scores*. The standard deviation is conceptually similar to the average deviation, but it is more useful because it is not always 0, and it has some interesting mathematical and statistical properties, which we discuss later. Remember, the standard deviation is always *from the mean*; the mean is the point of reference. How much are the scores deviating from the mean? What is the typical or standard deviation of scores from the mean? Let's consider the same set of numbers as before (1, 2, 3, 4, 5, 3, 3), and illustrate the computation of its standard deviation.

- Compute the *mean* as we did above; it better still be 3, but check it.

- Compute the *deviations from the mean*; subtract the mean from each score.

- Square each *deviation from the mean*; check these computations below:

- Sum the squared deviations:

$$\Sigma\,(\text{Score} - \text{Mean})^2 = (4 + 1 + 0 + 1 + 4 + 0 + 0) = 10.$$

- Divide the sum of squared deviations by the number of scores:

$$\Sigma\,(\text{Score} - \text{Mean})^2 / 7 = 10 / 7 = 1.43.$$

- Take the square root of the quotient to obtain the standard deviation: Square root of 1.43 = 1.196.

Deviation From the Mean (Score – Mean)	Deviation From the Mean Squared (Score – Mean)^2
$(1 - 3) = -2$	$(1 - 3)^2 = -2^2 = 4$
$(2 - 3) = -1$	$(2 - 3)^2 = -1^2 = 1$
$(3 - 3) = 0$	$(3 - 3)^2 = 0^2 = 0$
$(4 - 3) = 1$	$(4 - 3)^2 = 1^2 = 1$
$(5 - 3) = 2$	$(5 - 3)^2 = 2^2 = 4$
$(3 - 3) = 0$	$(3 - 3)^2 = 0^2 = 0$
$(3 - 3) = 0$	$(3 - 3)^2 = 0^2 = 0$

Hence, the standard deviation of this set of numbers is 1.196, and the formula is

$$\text{Standard Deviation } (SD) = \sqrt{\frac{\Sigma\,(\text{Score} - \text{Mean})^2}{N}}$$

One small note: Statisticians use the shorthand expression *sum of squares* to refer to the sum of the deviations from the mean squared, which often confuses students. So remember that you *square all the deviations from the mean* and then calculate the sum to get the sum of squares; then you divide by the number of scores and take the square root of this quotient to get the standard deviation. Now you have the formula for computing the standard deviation, but it is just as important to know what *standard deviation* means—the extent to which your set of scores vary from the mean—the larger the standard deviation, the more widely the scores vary from the mean (see Figure 3.1); when the standard deviation is small, the variability is also small.

Knowing the mean and the standard deviation of a group of scores gives you a better understanding of an individual score. For example, suppose you received a score of 79 on a test. You would be pleased with the score if the mean of the test were 70 and the *SD* were 4 because your score would be a little more than 2 *SD*s above the mean, a score well above average.

Consider the difference if the mean of the test had remained at 70, but the *SD* had been 16. In this case, your score of 79 would be less than 1 *SD* from the mean. You would be much closer to the middle of the group, with a score slightly above average, but not high. Knowing the standard deviation tells you much more than simply knowing the range of scores. No matter how the majority scored on the test, one or two students may do very well or very poorly and thus make the range very large.

NORMAL DISTRIBUTION

Standard deviations are especially useful if the distribution of scores is normal. You have heard of a **normal distribution** before; it is the bell-shaped curve that describes many naturally occurring physical and social phenomena, such as height and intelligence. Most scores in a normal distribution fall toward the middle, with fewer and fewer scores toward the ends, or the *tails*, of the distribution. The mean of a normal distribution is also its midpoint. Half the scores are above the mean, and half are below it. Furthermore, the mean, median, and mode are identical in a normal distribution.

As you can see in Figure 3.1, when the distribution of scores is normal, the percentage of scores falling within each area of the curve is known. Scores have a tendency toward the middle or mean. In fact, 68% of all scores are located in the area from 1 *SD* below to 1 *SD* above the mean. About 16% of the scores are beyond 1 *SD* above the mean. Of this higher group, only 2% are greater than 2 *SD*s above the mean. Similarly, only about 16% of the scores are beyond 1 *SD* below the mean, and of that group only about 2% are beyond 2 *SD*s below the mean.

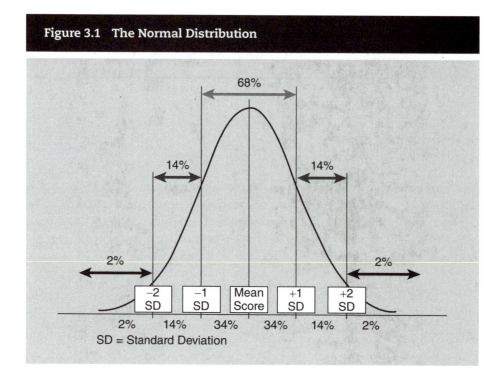

Figure 3.1 The Normal Distribution

68%

14%   14%

2%   2%

| −2 SD | −1 SD | Mean Score | +1 SD | +2 SD |

2%   14%   34%   34%   14%   2%

SD = Standard Deviation

Standard scores are based on the standard deviation. A **z score** *is a standard score that tells how many standard deviations above or below the mean a score falls.* In the example described earlier, where you were fortunate enough to get a 79 on a test where the mean was 70 and the *SD* was 4, your z score would have been greater than 2 *SD*s above the mean (actually 2.25 *SD*s above the mean), which means that your score is higher than 98% of those who took the test. To determine your place in a normal distribution, you need to convert your raw score to a standard score, which is a simple process—simply subtract the mean from the raw score and divide the difference by the standard deviation. The formula is

$$Z = \frac{\text{Raw score} - \text{Mean}}{\text{Standard deviation}}$$

POPULATIONS AND SAMPLES

So far, all our statistics have described properties of **populations**. The population, or universe, *contains all the elements of the set.* If you have all the elements of the set you are studying, for example, all the scores for all students in your class, then you have the results for that universe. You can compute the *exact* or actual mean, mode, median, range, and standard deviation for the population; there is no need to estimate.

For the most part, however, researchers are interested in samples of a population. A **sample** *is a subgroup of the population.* If we want to generalize about the third-grade students in the country, the population is all-third grade students in America. It is impractical, if not impossible, to get information on all such students, so researchers limit the population to third grade students in a state. Even this population may be too large for practical purposes, so we take a subgroup of these students as a sample. We would like to get a representative sample so that our conclusions are general to the population.

We need to add a few more refinements to our definitions because we are usually directly concerned with samples rather than populations. *Statistics are the characteristics of samples. Parameters are the characteristics of populations.* That is, measures of central tendencies (mean, mode, median) and indicators of variability (range and standard deviation) are parameters, which are estimated from the sample. One formula, the standard deviation, needs to be altered slightly to get a better estimate of the actual standard deviation of the population. In other words, when using a sample to estimate the standard deviation of a population, divide by $n - 1$ (number in the sample minus 1). This revised formula yields a better estimate of the standard deviation for the population; this slightly altered way of calculating the variance is called the mean square and has other mathematical and statistical properties that make it useful. Thus, the standard deviation for a sample is best defined as

$$SD = \sqrt{\frac{\sum(\text{score} - \text{Mean})^2}{n-1}}$$

Thus far in our analysis, we have used the standard deviation as a measure of the variability. A related concept that is more useful in statistics is the variance of a set of scores. The variance of a sample is its standard deviation squared.

$$\text{Variance } (V) = \frac{\sum(\text{score} - \text{Mean})^2}{n-1}$$

The variance and the mean are the two key concepts used in most statistical analyses. Both are summaries of a set of scores; the mean is a measure of central tendency and the variance a measure of variability. We started our discussion of variability with the standard deviation because we assumed that it was more familiar, but now the related concept of variance becomes our chief index of variability.

Much of statistical analysis is explaining the variance in the dependent variable. *Does the independent variable cause the dependent variable to vary or lean in a certain direction?* That is the key problem of inferential statistics. We ask the question "Were the results of my study a consequence of the independent variable, or were they a result of chance?"

In other words, we measure our actual findings against the chance model. We attempt to eliminate chance as an explanation of our results in order to buttress the argument that our independent variable, not chance, made the difference. To reiterate the central thesis of inferential statistics, "Did the results occur by chance, or are they a function of our independent variable?" Statistics and probability help us answer this basic question. This is not a book on statistics; however, a basic conceptual understanding of statistical tests is essential if we are to grasp the nature and meaning of quantitative research.

STATISTICAL TESTS

One more time, here is the *basic statistical question*: Is what I found in my research significantly different from what I would expect to find by chance? What you as a researcher need to do is to compare your actual results with the chance model. Do the results vary enough from chance to conclude that something else is causing the variance or variability in the dependent variable? Statistics provide critical ratios, such as the *t* ratio, the *F* ratio, or chi square, which enable us to answer the chance question with confidence (see "Elements of a Proposal," Appendix A).

t Test

All critical ratios work the same way, and we illustrate a few so that you understand what is happening and why. The *t* **test** is a good place to begin because it is a clear, straightforward statistical application. If we are doing a study in which the independent variable has only two categories and the dependent variable is continuous, then the appropriate statistic is a *t* test.

For example, suppose we want to know if college men and women are significantly different with respect to liberal attitudes toward premarital sex. Note that the population is all students at College A. Assume that we select a representative sample of men and women from College A, and we have all students in the sample respond to a reliable and valid scale measuring their attitudes. Assume further that the higher the score on the scale, the more liberal their attitudes. How can we test the results of our little research problem?

First, we divide the sample into two groups, male and female; the independent variable has only two categories. Then we compute the mean scores for men and for women on the dependent variable—liberal attitudes toward premarital sex. Finally, we ask whether the means for the men and women were significantly different. *The t test is an appropriate statistical procedure when the independent variable has two and only two categories and the dependent variable is continuous.*

Here is how the *t* test works. To assess whether there is a significant difference (one not explained by the chance model), we compare what we found—the *actual difference* in scores between men and women—with the *difference expected by chance*. The ratio between the actual difference and the difference due to chance is a *t* ratio. A *t* test is defined as

$$t = \frac{\text{Actual difference in the means}}{\text{Difference expected by chance}}$$

The larger the ratio, the greater the probability that the difference is not a function of chance. If the *t* **value** is 1, what does that mean? The actual difference between the means is exactly what to expect if nothing but chance is working; chance is explaining this relationship. But, if the *t* value is 2, it is more likely that something other than chance is operating.

Let's continue a little further without getting bogged down in statistical calculations. The general formula for a *t* test is as follows:

$$t = \frac{\text{Mean from Group 1} - \text{Mean from Group 2}}{\text{Standard error of the difference between the means of the two groups}}$$

There are several important aspects of this general formula:

1. We are examining the actual difference between the means of the two groups.

2. We are comparing the actual difference with what is expected by chance.

3. Statisticians can determine what is expected by chance by computing the standard error of the difference between the two means.

4. A *t* ratio is computed that indicates the extent to which the results depart from the chance model: The greater the *t* value, the greater the likelihood that chance is not explaining the relationship.

Fortunately for us, using any one of a number of statistical packages, the computer calculates the standard error of the difference between the means as well as the *t* ratio and its **level of significance** (*p* value).

A *p* **value** is a probability level that indicates the level of significance, that is, *the probability that the results are a function of chance*. When you read research publications, you find statements like ($t = 2.62, p < .01$). This means that a t test produced a t ratio of 2.62, which was significant beyond the .01 level of significance ($p < .01$); hence, we can be quite confident that the chance model does not explain the relationship. By convention, most researchers accept a relation as statistically significant if the p value is equal to or less than .05. What that means is that the relation could have occurred by chance only 5 times or less out of 100.

Let's return to the question of whether men and women at College A have different attitudes toward premarital sex.

- First, we add up all the scores for the men and divide by the number of men (mean score for men) and do the same for the women (mean score for women).

- Next, we subtract the scores (mean score of men minus mean score of women).

- Then, we compute the standard error of the difference between the means of men and women (the difference we would expect to get by chance).

- Finally, we compare the two by computing a t ratio (actual difference divided by the standard error of the difference).

Fortunately, our laptop and SPSS computer program does all this as quickly as we can hit the Execute button. The results include the t value and give us its level of significance.

What would it mean in our research project if we obtained the following: ($t = 1.02$, $p > .95$)? The answer is that a t value of 1.02 is not statistically significant. We can tell this just by looking at the t value because 1 would indicate perfect chance to explain the result. The $p > .95$ indicates that more than 95 times out of 100, chance would explain our results. Hence, in College A, we can conclude with great confidence that there is no significant difference between men and women in their attitudes toward premarital sex.

F Test

The independent variable is not always a dichotomous variable, one with only two categories. Sometimes the independent variable has more than two categories. If so, we cannot use the t test. We need a more general test that does essentially the same thing, that is, produces a critical ratio to check the departure from the chance model. In a case when there is more than two categories in the independent variable and a continuous dependent variable, the more general F ratio provides our answer. An F test is done using a statistical procedure called **analysis of variance (ANOVA)**. There are a variety of ANOVAs, and we now focus on the least complex; however, conceptually all ANOVAs are similar in that one or more *F* **values** are computed to answer the question of the deviation from the chance model question.

Let's illustrate a simple one-way ANOVA with an example. Suppose I want to test the effectiveness of three teaching approaches with graduate students in education—teacher directed, student directed, and shared. I am teaching a large group of 90 students in an introductory course in education, about a third of all the beginning graduate education students. *Does my teaching approach make any difference in the mastery of key concepts in education?* Assume that I can divide the group into three similar subgroups; probably the best way to do this is to assign the students to the groups at random. Assume further that the 90 students are representative of all beginning graduate education students at my university.

What is my independent variable in the research problem? How many independent variables do I have? Three? No, actually I have only one independent variable (teaching approach) with three variations or categories (teacher-directed, student-directed, and shared approaches). The independent variable is a manipulated categorical variable. I, the researcher, will manipulate the variable by teaching each group in one of three ways. What is the dependent variable? I am interested in mastery of basic education concepts, and I have a final exam that I developed over the years that is reliable and valid; that is, it taps the content that I am interested in having students master in a consistent manner. The dependent variable is measured by my test and is continuous: The higher the test score, the greater the level of mastery of basic concepts. *The F test is an appropriate statistical procedure when the independent variable has two or more categories and the dependent variable is continuous.*

Here is how an *F* test is computed using ANOVA. At the end of the term, I compute the mean score on mastery for each of the three groups. Almost certainly, there will be differences in the means, but the question is essentially the same here as it was for the *t* test: Is there a *significant* difference *among* the three mean scores? I proceed by doing the following:

- First, compute the mean for each of the three groups on the mastery exam.

- Next, calculate the total variance for the entire sample. That is, combine all three groups into one, and compute the overall mean for the entire 90 students. To compute the variance for the entire group, which is called the total variance (V_t), use the following formula described earlier:

$$\text{Variance}(V) = \frac{\sum(\text{score} - \text{Mean})^2}{n-1}$$

- Now compute the variance between the groups. To do this, we treat each of the three means for the groups as data points and use our variance formula. The **between-group variance** is the variance caused by the independent variable; it is also called **systematic or experimental variance**.

- The variance due to error is commonly called the **within-group variance**; it is also called **error variance**. This computation is a little more difficult to explain, but conceptually it is the variance "left over" from the total variance after the between-groups or experimental variance is removed from the total variance. The within-group variance is a measure of chance variation.

- Finally, calculate the F ratio, which is the variance produced by the independent variable divided by the variance due to chance.

$$F = \frac{\text{Variance due to the independent variable}}{\text{Variance due to change}} = \frac{\text{Between-groups variance}}{\text{Within-groups variance}}$$

We have come a long way to show that the F ratio using ANOVA is essentially the same as a t ratio in that both compare actual findings in relation to chance and yield an index and a probability level to enable us to make confident judgments about the nature of our relationships. A significant F ratio in this kind of problem simply means that there is a significant difference *among the three groups*. To find which pairs of means are different, we must do some further post hoc analyses, which can be found in any good statistics book. But, the idea is the same: *Compare your actual results with what you would expect by chance.*

Chi-Square Test

Sometimes, both the independent and the dependent variables are categorical. If so, we need another statistical tool called the **chi-square (χ^2) test** to compute the critical ratio for such situations. Suppose you want to examine the relationship between gender and graduation. *Is the gender of the students related to whether or not one graduates?* What are the independent and dependent variables of this research problem? What kind of variable is each in terms of measurement? Gender is the independent variable; it is the presumed cause and has two variations or categories: male and female. Graduation is the dependent variable, and it also has two categories: graduate and no graduate. One might also consider graduation as a continuous variable, that is, graduation rate, but to illustrate the chi-square, we cast graduation as a dichotomous variable.

We decide to go back to the freshman class of four years ago and see how many men and women graduated at the end of four years. We select a random sample of 100: 50 men and 50 women. We summarize the results of our research in a 2 × 2 cross break or contingency table (see Table 3.1).

Table 3.1 Summary of the Results of our Analysis

	Men	Women	
Graduate	15	35	50
No graduate	35	15	50
	50	50	100

As we examine the results in the 2 × 2 table, we see that in our sample, women may be more likely to graduate than men, but what is the likelihood that the results can be explained by chance? In other words, we need to *compare what we found in this analysis with what we would expect to find by chance*. Do the results here represent a major departure from the chance model? We need a critical ratio. *The chi-square test is the appropriate statistic when both variables are categorical.* The chi-square is a test of frequency counts. What do the numbers in the cells of our 2 × 2 table represent? Yes, frequencies—the number of students in each cell. The chi-square is an index of the actual results compared with those expected by chance. Examine the formula for chi-square:

$$\text{Chi-square}\,(\chi^2) = \Sigma \left[\frac{(f_0 - f_e)^2}{f_e} \right]$$

Now, we use the formula and the previous results obtained and summarized in our 2 × 2 cross break. The chance model would predict 25 students in each cell; that is, the expected frequency for each cell (f_e) is 25. Now compare the expected with the actual for each cell by subtracting the expected frequency (f_e) from the observed frequency (f_o), squaring the difference, and then dividing the difference by the expected frequency (f_e). Let's do the computations for each cell and sum them as the formula instructs.

$$\chi^2 = [(15 - 25)^2/25] + [(35 - 25)^2/25] + [(15 - 25)^2/25] + [(35 - 25)^2/25]$$

$$\chi^2 = [100/25] + [100/25] + [100/25] + [100/25]$$

$$\chi^2 = 4 + 4 + 4 + 4$$

$$\chi^2 = 16.$$

The χ^2 index is 16. What would the chi-square have been if only chance were working? Each cell would have had the number 25, and χ^2 would have been 0. Run the numbers, and make sure you see why the answer is 0. Thus, our index of departure from chance in this example is 16. Using a computer program, we would have found ($\chi^2 = 16$, $p <.01$). The results show that a χ^2 of 16 is statistically significant beyond the .01 level of significance; that is, these results would occur by chance less than 1 time out of 100. Our conclusion would be that women are more likely to graduate from the college than are men. Note that, as always, our conclusion is probabilistic, not certain. The point of this exercise is to demonstrate the meaning of yet another critical ratio, one that works when both variables are categorical.

Effect Size

The three tests that we examined thus far—the *t* test, the *F* test, and chi-square— are statistics that help us answer the basic statistical question: *Is what I found in my analysis significantly different than I would expect to find by chance?* None of these statistics, however, tells us anything about the magnitude of the relation. Increasingly, researchers want to know the strength of the relation, that is, its **effect size**. *The magnitude of the independent variable's effect on the dependent variable is the effect size.* Suffice it to say that when using *t* tests, analysis of variance, or chi-square analysis, we must do additional computations to determine effect size. For example, a contingency coefficient and an omega-squared (Hays, 1994; Kerlinger & Lee, 2000) are relatively straightforward computations that will tell us the magnitude of the effect size. The point here is that the *F* and *t* values and chi-square tell us if there is a statistically significant relationship, but they do not indicate the magnitude of the relation; other indices are needed.

We turn next to coefficients of correlation, which not only answer the question of statistical significance, but also indicate the magnitude of the relationship between the independent and dependent variable—the proportion of variance in the dependent variable explained by the independent variable. Correlation coefficients, unlike the statistics explored thus far, answer *both* the statistical significance and the effect size questions.

Linear Regression and Coefficient of Correlation

What if both the independent and the dependent variables are continuous? We need another statistic: A **coefficient of correlation (*r*)** will give us the answer to whether the relation is likely a chance one or not. But, another useful feature of the correlation is that we can use it to test not only the departure from the chance model, but also the strength of the relation. A coefficient of correlation *is a number that indicates the magnitude of the relation between two continuous variables such that the higher the absolute value of the correlation, the stronger the relation.* Correlations range in value from −1 to +1. If the two variables vary together, they have a positive correlation, which means that as the value of one increases, so does the other. If the correlation is negative, then as the independent variable changes, the dependent variable changes in the opposite direction. Which is stronger, a correlation of +1 or one of -1? Neither. Both are perfect correlations; both are as high as they can get, but in opposite directions. The sign of the correlation represents the direction of the relation and has nothing to do with its strength. So $r = -.85$ is a stronger correlation than $r = +.41$ because the sign merely indicates whether the variables are varying in the same or opposite direction.

The calculations of coefficients of correlations are a little more tedious and not as self-evident as the other statistics that we have discussed, so we will not spend much time with the formulas and computations. Instead, we illustrate the correlations with a table. Correlations describe linear relations, which are straight lines when graphed. The relation between two variables, *x* and *y*, is a set of ordered pairs. That means that for every value of *x* there is one corresponding value of *y*. We can express the pairs of values in set notation, or we can simply express them in a table or graph or both. Consider the relations between *three* sets of ordered pairs (relations) as expressed in Table 3.2.

The first set of ordered pairs (1) has a correlation coefficient of +1; the numbers vary together. For each change in the independent variable *x*, there is a corresponding change in the dependent variable *y* of the same magnitude and direction. In the second set of ordered pairs (2), sometimes a change in *x* produces a positive change in *y* and sometimes a negative change; there is no systematic pattern in the relation; there is no relation ($r = 0$). Finally, in the third set (3), for each change in *x* there is a corresponding change in *y* of the same magnitude except in the opposite direction; we have a perfect **negative correlation** ($r = -1$); *x* and *y* vary together in opposite directions. In brief, the correlation coefficient provides an index of the extent to which the two variables vary together and the direction of the variation.

A computer program will provide you with correlation coefficients and levels of significance. Consider the statement ($r = -.52, p < .01$). The correlation is negative:

Table 3.2 Correlations for Three Sets of Numbers

(1) r = 1.00		(2) r = 0		(3) r = −1.00	
x	y	x	y	x	y
1	1	1	2	1	5
2	2	2	5	2	4
3	3	3	3	3	3
4	4	4	1	4	2
5	5	5	4	5	1

As x increases, y decreases. The relation is statistically significant; that is, chance is unlikely to explain the relationship; in fact, in less than 1 time in 100, the two variables would not be related. The correlation coefficient also suggests how strong the relation is between the two variables. Square the coefficient of correlation and multiply it by 100, and you have an estimate of the percentage of the variance in the dependent variable (y) caused by the independent variable (its effect size). For example, if $r = .50$, then the independent variable x explains 25% of the variance in y. If $r = 0$, then none of the variance in y is explained by x. If $r = −.83$, then about 69% of the variance in y is explained by x. An important point: *What scientists try to do with their research and statistics is to identify independent variables that explain the variance in the dependent variable.* Explaining variance in a dependent variable is an important goal of scientific research.

A final observation about a correlation coefficient—it is mathematically the coefficient of x in the formula for a straight line, as expressed by the following equation:

$$y = mx + b.$$

Think of the set of ordered pairs that represents the relation between the independent variable, x, and the dependent variable, y, as a graph of a line that passes through those points such that the line represents the best fit for all the points; mathematically, that means the sum of all the distances from the points to the line (sometimes called a regression line) would be as small as possible. If we standardize x and y, then the coefficient of x is the correlation coefficient for the regression line for the relation of x and y. In sum, a correlation coefficient for a relation in which both variables have been standardized is the slope of its regression line. The regression line for two variables will take the form of $y = mx + b$, where m is the slope of the line and the correlation coefficient for the standardized data and b is the y-intercept. Perhaps we are getting a little too technical, so let's move on.

Multiple Regression and
Multiple Coefficient of Correlation

Thus far, all the tests that we describe are bivariate; that is, they examine the relation between *one independent and one dependent variable*. In the actual world, relationships are more complicated. Typically, dependent variables are influenced by more than one variable at a time; thus, we need multivariate statistics. You should be beginning to realize that there are statistics for just about any relation you can imagine, but most are designed to answer basic questions: Can I reject the chance model as a good explanation? How strong is this relationship?

Just as a simple correlation (r) tells us whether the chance model can be rejected and how strong the relation is between x and y, a **multiple correlation (R)** tells us the same thing. But, in the case of the multiple R we have a little more information because *R represents how much variance in the continuous dependent variable y is explained by a set of continuous independent variables ($x_1, x_2, x_3 \ldots x_n$)*. Moreover, each x variable has a coefficient, which is sometimes called a regression coefficient or **beta weight**. So, a multiple regression analysis produces a multiple R, which represents the combined influence of all the independent variables on the dependent variable y, as well as a regression coefficient or beta weight for each independent variable (x). The coefficients represent the strength of the relation between that x and the dependent y, controlling for the other xs—that is, taking out the influence of the other independent variables. Consider the following formula for a multiple regression line:

$$y = ax_1 + bx_2 + cx_3 + i \text{ (the intercept)}.$$

Note that this equation is simply an extension of simple regression; multiple regression is an extension of simple regression where there are multiple independent variables predicting a single dependent variable. In the regression equation above, we have three independent variables instead of only one. For example, we might be trying to predict student achievement (y) based on the IQ (x_1), motivation (x_2), and sense of optimism (x_3) of students. If we had data from some sample of students on these variables, we could use a standard statistical package to run a multiple regression analysis on this set of variables. The analysis would first compute an R, which would tell us how strong the relation is between this set of variables and student achievement. For example, what is the combined impact of IQ, motivation, and sense of optimism on student achievement? If we square the R, then R^2 is a good estimate of how much of the variance in student achievement is explained by the combination of IQ, motivation, and sense of optimism. The program also computes a t value or F ratio to gauge the likelihood that the relation is a matter of chance. Furthermore, the analysis yields a standardized beta coefficient for each independent variable, which tells us how much influence each independent variable has relative to the other independent variables, and, of course, for each coefficient there will be a corresponding test to determine its departure from chance.

Remember that the two variables in simple correlation are both continuous; this is also the case in multiple regression—all the variables are typically continuous.

Hierarchical Linear Modeling (HLM)

HLM is simply multiple regression performed with hierarchical data, data that are clustered or nested within different units of analysis. For example, in school effects research, students are nested in schools. There are two different levels of analysis: the individual (students) and the school.

Why use HLM if it is just multiple regression? Let's go back to the purpose of multiple regression—to test the relationship among a set of independent variables and a single dependent variable. But, what if the question is how important is the school versus the individual in influencing some dependent variable? HLM enables us to answer this question efficiently. A standard multiple regression analysis of student achievement across schools does not simultaneously account for both student and school effects; HLM does.

To estimate a school effect in standard multiple regression, the researcher needs to aggregate individual student data to the school level by calculating a mean student score for each school. In the process of aggregating, however, we lose the differential effect of individual students on the dependent variable. So, how does HLM differ? Let's say we are interested in the relationship between collective faculty trust in students and student achievement. This question involves hierarchical data because student achievement is measured at the individual student level, but collective faculty trust is measured as a school property. Students are nested in schools; therefore, it is necessary to separate the variance in student achievement due to differences in schools and differences in individual students. In our example, we might find that 20% of the variance in student achievement is attributed to school differences while the other 80% is due to individual differences or to chance.

Remember the purpose of research is to explain the variance of a dependent variable, in this case achievement. There are several student factors that may explain differences in student achievement at the individual student level. Likewise, there are many school factors that may explain achievement differences across schools. We need to include these multiple variables in the regression model. In our example, we might use a measure of SES (socioeconomic status) as well as IQ at the individual level, and a measure of school poverty along with collective faculty trust at the school level. With this model, we now are accounting for achievement differences due to student SES, IQ, school poverty, and collective trust of the faculty. In this case, the four independent variables are student SES, IQ, school poverty, and collective faculty trust. Note that the independent variables are at different levels—student SES and IQ are individual variables while school poverty and collective faculty trust are school variables. The reason we use HLM is because the multiple independent variables are at two different levels.

Thus far, our analyses focused on examining the relations between independent variables and one dependent variable. When statistical analyses simultaneously test relations among *both* multiple independent and multiple dependent variables, the procedures are called multivariate. We could continue building our set of statistical procedures. For example, what if we are interested in multiple independent variables and multiple dependent variables? There are, of course, statistical tests for such circumstances, multivariate analysis of variance (MANOVA), canonical correlation, and structural equation modeling (SEM). But, we have gone far enough to give you a flavor of statistics, what they do, and when and how they are employed.

SUMMARY

If you have carefully read and studied this chapter, you now have a good working repertoire of statistical procedures and tests; however, the chapter is not a substitute for a set of statistics courses, but it should provide the conceptual understanding that you need to begin to analyze and frame quantitative research. Let's review the key points:

- The mean, mode, and median are measures of central tendencies.

- The range and standard deviation are measures of variability.

- The basic purpose of inferential statistics is to answer the question "Were the results of my study a consequence of the independent variable, or were they a result of chance?"

- Your inventory of statistical tests includes

  o the *t* test for the difference between two means,

  o ANOVA and the *F* test,

  o the chi-square test,

  o coefficients of correlation (r),

  o multiple regression and multiple correlations (R), and

  o hierarchical linear modeling (HLM).

- Which test is appropriate depends on the nature of the independent and dependent variables, that is, whether they are continuous or categorical and nested or not (see Table 3.3 for a summary).

Table 3.3 Types of Variables and Appropriate Statistical Tests

Independent Variable	Dependent Variable	Statistical Test
Dichotomous	Continuous	*t* test
Categorical	Continuous	*F* test (ANOVA)
Categorical	Categorical	Chi-square (χ^2)
Continuous	Continuous	Correlation (*r*)
Multiple and continuous	Continuous	Multiple correlation (*R*)
Multiple, continuous, and nested	Continuous	Hierarchical Linear Modeling (HLM)

CHECK YOUR UNDERSTANDING

1. An educational researcher conducted an experiment with two groups: an experimental group (A) and a control group (B). A was a taught using "dynamic inquiry," and B was taught in a traditional way. At the end of the unit, a performance test was given to both groups, and their scores were as follows:

   A   B

   3   6

   5   5

   1   7

   4   8

   2   4

   Using the formulas in this chapter, compute the mean, standard deviation, and variance for Group A and Group B. Based on the results, develop a hypothesis relating dynamic inquiry and effectiveness.

2. The following scores are the result of a test of reading comprehension in a fourth grade class:

   0, 2, 4, 1, 3, 5, 2, 4, 6, 6, 4, 2, 5, 3, 1, 4, 2, 0

   What are the mean, mode, and median for this set of scores? What are the range, average deviation, and standard deviation? In your own *words*, not in statistical terms, describe the variance and central tendency of this distribution.

3. A student score of 600 on the SAT (Scholastic Aptitude Test) is the same as a standard score of 1. How does this student compare with all those who have taken the test? What if the SAT score is 300 or a standard score of -2? What is a standard score? (*Hint:* For the SAT test, the mean score is 500, and $SD = 100$.)

4. Compute a *t* value for Exercise 1 above, assuming that the standard error of the difference between the two means is 1. Interpret what that *t* value means. Is the difference in the means of the two groups statistically significant?

5. You computed a correlation between the socioeconomic status of your students and their math achievement scores ($r = .70$). Interpret what this correlation means. If this is a true correlation, what can you as a teacher do to improve performance? How much does SES help or hinder your task?

6. You just read an interesting article where the researcher shows that the multiple regression of home background (HB), intelligence (IQ), and motivation (M) on achievement produces an R^2 of .87 and the standardized beta weights are .31, .41, and .34, respectively. How strong is the relation? Which variable is the most important in explaining achievement? What is the relative influence of each of the independent variables? What conclusions can you draw?

7. A school district wants to examine the influence of academic optimism on student achievement. Data are collected for academic optimism of the schools, the socioeconomic status of students, the attendance record of students, and the mathematics achievement of students. What are the independent variables? Dependent variable? School-level variables? Individual-level variables? What kind of analysis is required? Why?

KEY TERMS

ANOVA (analysis of variance) (p. 55)
Beta weight (p. 61)
Between-group variance (p. 56)
Chi-square (χ^2) (p. 56)
Coefficient of correlation (r) (p. 59)
Effect size (p. 58)
Error variance (p. 56)
Experimental variance (p. 56)

F value (p. 55)
Hierarchical linear modeling (HLM) (p. 62)
Level of significance (p. 53)
Mean (p. 45)
Median (p. 45)
Mode (p. 45)
Multiple correlation (R) (p. 61)
Multiple regression (p. 61)
Negative correlation (p. 59)
Normal distribution (p. 49)

Population (p. 50)
p Value (p. 53)
Range (p. 47)
Research hypothesis (p. 000)
Sample (p. 51)
Standard deviation (p. 47)
Standard score (p. 50)
Systematic variance (p. 56)
t Test (p. 52)
t Value (p. 53)
Within-group variance (p. 56)
z Score (p. 50)

4

ANALYZING THE STRUCTURE AND SUBSTANCE OF HYPOTHESES

We turn to hypotheses in this chapter. What is a hypothesis? What are the criteria of a **good hypothesis**? We build on our understanding of variables and focus on relations between variables in the form of hypotheses. We examine the notions of **"theoretical hypotheses"** or "substantive hypotheses" and **"statistical hypotheses,"** such as a **"null hypothesis."** We explore simple hypotheses as well as more complex ones. Our goal is to diagram hypotheses in the way that a grammarian diagrams sentences. We begin by defining a hypothesis and its elements. Then we conclude by constructing a framework for diagramming hypotheses and applying it to multiple hypotheses. Oh yes, we also apply the statistical knowledge we learned in the previous chapter to our analysis of hypotheses.

HYPOTHESES

We concluded the second chapter by defining a research problem as *a query that asks what the relationship is between two or more variables.* Typically, researchers begin their work with scientific problems, that is, questions about relations between variables. For example, what is the relationship between bureaucratic structure and teacher sense of alienation? Not all questions, however, are scientific questions. Consider the question "What makes a good principal?" Although the question may be interesting to you, it is not a scientific problem because it is not a question of the relationship between variables. Contrast this query with the following question: "What is the relation between administrative drive and organizational effectiveness?" In the last interrogative, we have the rough beginnings of a research problem because it deals with the relationship between two variables—administrative drive and organizational effectiveness.

Studies begin with research questions, are transformed and guided by hypotheses, and culminate with the testing of the hypotheses. Problems and questions need answers. A hypothesis is the proposed answer to a research problem. To be more specific, a hypothesis *is a conjectural statement that indicates the relationship between at least two variables*. Hypotheses are conjectures; they specify how the variables relate to each other (see "Elements of a Proposal," Appendix A). Note the following essential characteristics of good hypotheses:

- They are *declarative statements*, not questions.

- They are *tentative*—conjectures that await empirical evidence.

- They must have at least two variables.

- They must be *testable*.

- They are statements of the *relation between variables*.

Hypotheses are usually more specific than research problems because in the search for responses to the questions, researchers examine the literature, conceptualize the problem, and specify their concepts (see "Elements of a Proposal," Appendix A, for an outline of this process in a dissertation proposal). In answer to the question "What is the relationship between bureaucratic structure and teacher sense of alienation?" the researcher might generate the following two hypotheses:

> *H.1:* Schools with a hindering bureaucratic structure have a greater sense of faculty powerlessness than schools with an **enabling structure**.

> *H.2:* Schools with a hindering bureaucratic structure have a greater sense of faculty meaninglessness than schools with an enabling structure.

These are both answers to the same general research question, but they are more specific than the research question because they suggest the conceptual schemes used to capture the meaning of bureaucratic structure (hindering vs. enabling structures) and alienation (powerlessness and meaninglessness). Note also that the hypotheses are written in the present tense and they relate concepts, not measures.

There are many ways to express hypotheses. Consider the following as illustrative: If *x*, then *y*; *x* causes *y*; *x* and *y* covary; *x* facilitates *y*; *x* is related to *y*; as *x* increases, *y* increases; and *y* is a function of *x*. There are many other ways to state the hypothesis, but the important point is that you need to *select the form of the hypothesis statement that best fits your variables and your study*. Without a very strong theory, you would be well advised not to state the hypothesis as a direct casual relation (*x* causes *y*). Instead, the hypothesis might be stated as a relational one such that the greater x, the greater y. Causation is a complex, thorny issue, which is well beyond the scope of this book. Be careful not to claim direct causation without strong reason and evidence.

In summary, a good hypothesis has a number of features; make certain that your hypothesis incorporates them:

- The hypothesis must have at least two variables.

- The hypothesis must specify a relation between the variables.

- The hypothesis must be testable.

- The hypothesis should be written in the present tense.

- The hypothesis should be conceptual—relate concepts, not measures.

- The hypothesis should be stated simply and clearly (see "A Few Writing Tips," Appendix B).

One final thought—the best hypotheses are derived from theory; they are deduced from theory as a way to test empirically a theoretical explanation. Theories are heuristic: They suggest many propositions that are in need of examination. Thus, good theories are your best source for generating sound hypotheses. As you grapple with your research problem, seek theories that spread light on the concepts that you are interested in studying.

KINDS OF HYPOTHESES

Just as there are many ways to classify variables, there are also a variety of kinds of hypotheses. One distinction that is useful is between substantive hypotheses and statistical hypotheses. The substantive hypothesis *is the statement of the hypothesis in conceptual or theoretical terms; a declarative statement describes the relation between the concepts or variables.* All the hypotheses illustrated thus far are substantive hypotheses, which are also called theoretical or research hypotheses.

Eventually, however, we will want to test our theoretical hypotheses. To test them, we must transform them into statistical hypotheses; that is, we *specify each hypothesis in terms of the measures of the variables.* There are two forms of the statistical hypothesis—the null and the alternative. The null hypothesis states that *there is no relation between the measures of the variables.* For example, if we are predicting that the students taught using a discovery approach will achieve at a higher level than those taught using a lecture approach, then our null hypothesis would take the following statistical form indicating a chance model explanation—no difference between the means of the two groups:

Null hypothesis: M_d (mean of discovery approach) = M_l (mean of lecture approach).

The directed, **alternative hypothesis** would take the following statistical form

Directed alternative: $M_d > M_l$.

The directed, alternative hypothesis predicts that the mean score for the group taught by the discovery approach is significantly higher than the mean score of the group taught using the lecture approach.

You know from the previous chapter, however, that statistics are used to reject the chance model. That is, statistical tests are used to reject the null hypothesis. Depending on the nature of the variables, the null hypothesis can take the form $M_a = M_b$, $r = 0$, χ^2 is not significant, t is not significant, F is not significant, and so on. If the null hypothesis (chance model) is rejected, then we are in a position to accept the directed, alternative hypothesis. We repeat—you can only use statistics to reject the null in anticipation of accepting the predicted alternative. Regardless of how the hypothesis is stated, it is the null hypothesis that is tested statistically. Remember—rejecting the null hypothesis supports the alternative hypothesis.

IMPOSTER AND MISCONCEIVED HYPOTHESES

There are many traps that must be avoided by students as they both read the research and develop their own hypotheses. Many hypotheses are poorly constructed, vague, misleading, and sometimes not really hypotheses (see Charters, 1992).

Imposters: Only One Variable

One occasionally finds in the literature, but more often in dissertations, statements that masquerade as hypotheses. Let's consider some imposters. One student recently came to me proud to present his original hypothesis: *Charismatic educational leaders make a difference in American schools.* At first blush, the statement may seem like a reasonable beginning hypothesis, but it is not. Although it is a declarative statement, what are the two variables? Charismatic leadership style might be a variable, but what is the other variable? Difference is not a variable. Different in what respect? We need a second variable to make this statement a legitimate hypothesis. If there are not at least two variables, then it is not a hypothesis.

Consider the following statement: *High school principals of this state rarely focus their attentions on school safety*. Again, what are the two variables? The extent to which principals spend time on school safety might be one variable, but that is the only variable. Here is yet another example of the same ilk. The researcher proposes to test the hypothesis that American public schools have cultures of pessimism. The degree of pessimism in the school culture might be a variable, but what is the other variable? Finally, consider the following proposal: The purpose of this research is to test the hypothesis that *New Jersey school boards are composed of professionals rather than nonprofessionals*. A descriptive study might be able to address this proposition, but it is no hypothesis because it does not examine the relation between two or more variables.

Incomplete Hypotheses: Something Missing

Some propositions offered as hypotheses are simply incomplete. The statements do not give us enough information to decide what the second variable is—even though a second variable is implied. For example, consider the following:

> Administrative teams with appointed leaders have more cohesion among team members.

The statement suggests that appointed leader teams have more cohesion than what—than teams with elected leaders? Than leaderless teams? Than nonappointed leader teams? This statement can be readily transformed into a hypothesis with two clearly identifiable variables, but as it stands now, it does not pass muster. There is no excuse for this kind of slipshod writing; in fact, it likely shows carelessness in writing, a lack of understanding of a hypothesis, or fuzzy thinking—none of which bodes well for the research. Take a minute and develop a good hypothesis using the concepts implied in this description of administrative teams.

Here is a similar example: *Elementary teachers are more humanistic in American schools*. Again, the problem is one of comparison. Clearly the dependent variable is the degree of humanism, but what is the independent variable? We don't know what or whom to compare the elementary teachers with—is it secondary teachers or principals, or is it a comparison of American and Russian schools or some other set of schools? Let's take the statement and develop some clear hypotheses. Consider the following:

> *H.3:* Elementary teachers are more humanistic than secondary teachers in American schools.

H.4: Elementary teachers are more humanistic than their principals in American schools.

H.5: Elementary teachers are more humanistic in American schools than their counterparts are in Russian schools.

You probably can figure out what the researcher means in a great many cases if you read the work and carefully examine the statistical analysis and discussion, but it should not be this difficult or ambiguous. Then again, sometimes you find that the researcher really does not have a hypothesis and is simply describing the character of American schools, in which case there are not two variables, and you are confronted with an imposter hypothesis.

Tautologies: Nothing New

In too many cases, what appear to be hypotheses are nothing more than **tautologies**; that is, they are of the variety "if *x*, then *x*." The independent and dependent variables are the same. Consider the following statement: *Teachers who are alienated are dissatisfied.* Can it be any other way? Is not alienation a form of dissatisfaction? The proposition appears to have two variables—alienation and satisfaction—but in the end, they are both descriptions of the same general state. The statement tells us nothing new; hence, it is a tautology, not a hypothesis.

Sometimes the research uses two different words to refer to the same property and claims a relation. In the example above, it is easy to see the tautology, but in other cases it is more difficult. For example, I once had a student who developed the perfectly reasonable theoretical hypothesis that *the more hierarchical the school structure, the greater the sense of powerlessness of the teachers.* Check this hypothesis—a declarative statement, two variables, clearly stated, a relation, and testable. It seems that it has all the criteria of a good hypothesis. Yet in the end, the statement turned out to be a tautology and not a hypothesis. How could that be, you ask. Clearly, the hypothesis seemed to have "the right stuff," yet it was a tautology. Examine the operational measures for each variable, and you find the flaw. In this case, the operational measures turned out to be composed of items that were virtually the same for the two concepts. Here is a tip: If the correlation between two variables is very high (above .90), then check to see how the measures of the two variables differ. Don't be surprised if the variables are masquerading as different properties, but in reality are the same property with different names—a tautology by any other name.

Unspecified and Untestable Hypotheses

Sometimes, declarative statements express a relationship between two variables, but the relation cannot be tested because it is unspecified. For example, consider the following relation: *Teacher loyalty is a function of the personality of the principal*. Let us examine this proposed hypothesis more closely. Personality is a variable, but what are the types of personality? How does personality vary? Along a continuum? By category? What are the categories of personality? As the hypothesis is stated, it cannot be tested; furthermore, it is difficult to understand just what the researcher is proposing; it is too vague. Moreover, are we to expect a positive or negative relation? Just what is the prediction? It is hard to tell. Unspecified relations or hypotheses where the categories of the variables are unknown obfuscate rather than guide. Consider the following hypotheses based on the unspecified relation above:

> *H.6:* Principals who are extroverts have more loyal faculties than those who are introverts.

> *H.7:* Open-minded principals have more loyal faculties than do closed-minded principals.

Note that these hypotheses specify the categories of personality and transform the unspecified relation between personality and loyalty into two testable hypotheses; in fact, the two are quite different.

Unspecified hypotheses are common. Here are a few more examples for your consideration. Turn them into testable hypotheses.

- The racial composition of the community is an important factor in determining the success of elections to raise tax levies.

- Faculty morale is positively related to the type of authority structure of the institution.

- The effectiveness of resident dorm counselors is dependent on the social relations that they have with resident students.

In sum, make sure that the hypotheses have two variables and clearly describe the relation between the variables. Beware of tautologies. Finally, make sure that the hypotheses are specified and can be tested.

FINDING HYPOTHESES IN RESEARCH STUDIES

In the next chapter, we discuss how to generate original hypotheses, but here we are concerned with finding and analyzing hypotheses in the research literature. One would think that is no problem, but often it is an issue. About half the research articles in education do not state the hypotheses clearly. You have to dig to find them, and most often you have to construct them yourself! Look for the statement of the purpose. What are the variables of the study, and how are they measured? Which are the independent variables, and which are dependent variables? Look for the reasoning that leads to the analysis. What statistics are used? Look at the conclusions in the discussion. What propositions are proposed in the discussion? We will shortly present a framework for diagramming hypotheses that organizes these questions and leads you to the hypotheses. Even if the hypotheses are explicitly stated, as Charters (1992) warns, don't count on them having a proper structure.

Good hypotheses are clear guides that direct your reading of the research. Among other things, they suggest how the variables are conceptualized and measured; they underscore a body of related literature; they lead to the correct study design; they suggest appropriate statistics for the analysis; and in general, they provide a useful direction by focusing on the important aspects of the study—what the study is all about (see "Elements of a Proposal," Appendix A).

ANALYZING AND DIAGRAMMING HYPOTHESES

After we find the hypothesis of a study, we need to conduct a careful and comprehensive analysis of it, which includes the following:

- Identify the independent and dependent variables by name.

- Determine the variable type—categorical or continuous.

- Elaborate each variable (**elaboration**)—What do the numbers mean?

- Specify the relation of the hypothesis (**specification**)—How are the variables related?

- Decide on the appropriate unit of analysis—What is the object of the study?

- Select the appropriate statistical test—What statistic do I use to test the null?

These items provide the elements of a framework and schema for analyzing and diagramming hypotheses (see Table 4.1). The schema builds on and refines the framework first introduced by Charters (1992) to dissect hypotheses.

Case I: Dichotomous Independent Variable and Continuous Dependent Variable

What are the independent and dependent variables that form the hypothesis? What is the presumed causal (independent) variable and presumed effect (dependent) variable? Which variable is "manipulated" or changed to examine its impact on the dependent variable? What are the names of each variable, and how is each conceptualized? This is the first set of questions in need of answers. I suggest that you clearly write down the hypothesis and then begin your analysis by answering the preceding questions.

Let's illustrate the process with the first hypothesis proposed in this chapter.

> *H.1:* Schools with a hindering bureaucratic structure have a greater sense of faculty powerlessness than do schools with an enabling structure.

This hypothesis is clearly stated, and so the identification and names of the variables are straightforward. The hypothesis suggests that the independent variable (*x*) is *bureaucratic structure* and the dependent variable (*y*) is *sense of powerlessness*. It is reasonable to assume that bureaucratic structure influences powerlessness. So far so good!

What kind of variable is each? This is an important question because the answer explains why we have two variables and not three. Beginning students often get confused with this kind of hypothesis, thinking that there are three variables (hindering, enabling, and powerlessness) when there are only two variables (bureaucratic structure and powerlessness). The independent variable, bureaucratic structure, is a categorical variable, whereas the dependent variable is a continuous variable.

As we elaborate each variable, it becomes clear why there are only two variables. Bureaucratic structure has two categories, hindering and enabling; that is, there are only two variations of structure. The dependent variable, powerlessness, is a continuous variable that varies along a continuum such that the higher the number, the greater the sense of powerlessness. It is important to make sure that a high number means what you think it means. In this case, we are claiming that the higher the score on the powerlessness variable, the greater the powerlessness.

A good rule for stating hypotheses is to *make sure that the numerical value of the variable is consistent with the name of the variable*; that is, the higher the value of the variable, the more of the property it has. In this case, the name of the variable is *sense of powerlessness*, and so a high value should mean more powerlessness. The same measure of powerlessness could be used as a measure of sense of power, in which a small value would represent a large sense of power. The key point is to be sure that the value of the

Table 4.1 Hypothesis Diagramming Table		
Research Hypotheses:		
	Independent Variable (x) [Presumed Cause]	Dependent Variable (y) [Presumed Effect]
Name of variable:		
Kind of variable: (Continuous or categorical)		
Elaboration of variable:		
Specify relationship:		
Unit of analysis: (Object of study)		
Null hypothesis:		
Statistical test of null hypothesis:		

measure and the name of the variable are running the same way. When you construct a hypothesis, make sure that the name of the variable and its measure are consistent; that is, the higher the value, the more of the property; this practice is good form.

Next, we make sure that we understand the unit of analysis. This can be a little tricky sometimes. In this case, we are claiming that the school is our object of study. We are concerned with the relation between structure and powerlessness. Let's explain the consequences of such a claim. We are studying and measuring school properties here. One school gives us one data point for each variable. Thus, School A has one score on bureaucratic structure (either a hindering or an enabling structure) and one score on faculty sense of powerlessness. In other words, the dependent variable is a school score, not an individual score. Even though we ask teachers to respond, we have one school score on powerlessness, which is an average score for the school. To repeat, the school score is what we are concerned with, not individual scores per se. When researchers study school properties, both the independent and the dependent variables are school properties because the unit of analysis is the school.

Finally, what is the null hypothesis that we are trying to reject? The directed hypothesis says that the mean powerlessness score for hindering structures will be greater than the mean powerlessness score for enabling structures; therefore, the

Table 4.2 Diagram of H.1

Research hypothesis H.1: *Schools with a hindering bureaucratic structure have a greater sense of faculty powerlessness than do schools with an enabling structure.*

	Independent Variable (*x*)	Dependent Variable (*y*)
Name of variable:	Bureaucratic structure	Sense of powerlessness
Kind of variable: (Continuous or categorical)	Categorical	Continuous
Elaboration of variable:	Hindering (*H*) or enabling (*E*)	Varies from low to high
Specify relationship:	For powerlessness: H > E	
Unit of analysis: (Object of study)	School	
Null hypothesis:	Mean of H = Mean of E	
Statistical test to reject the null:	*t* test or *F* test	

null hypothesis is that the two means will be the same; that is, there is no difference. The appropriate statistical test of the null is either a *t* test or an *F* test. The complete diagram of the hypothesis is summarized in Table 4.2.

This diagram contains the elements that you need for a careful and systematic analysis of a hypothesis. It is a guide that you should commit to memory. Use the diagram as you analyze hypotheses in this chapter. One suggestion: When you elaborate a variable or specify the relations, use shorthand descriptions that you understand. Understanding is the key. Don't let the symbols confuse you. In this diagram, you could have just as easily used the statement "Powerlessness is greater in hindering than enabling structures."

Case II: Continuous Independent and Continuous Dependent Variables

To illustrate a hypothesis with two continuous variables, consider the following:

(H.1a) *The greater the degree of hindering bureaucratic structure in schools, the greater is the sense of faculty powerlessness.* This hypothesis describes the same relationship as the previous one; that is, the concepts are the same—bureaucratic structure and powerlessness—but the statement clearly implies that both variables are continuous. Table 4.3 presents the diagram of this hypothesis. Compare Tables 4.2 and 4.3.

The two hypotheses (H.1 and H.1a) capture the same relation between x and y, and the unit of analysis is the same; however, the independent variable in H.1a is continuous and varies from low to high, and thus the relation is specified differently. The null hypothesis is tested by a correlation coefficient and not an F or a t test. Study the two hypotheses and their diagrams (Tables 4.2 and 4.3) to make sure you understand the difference.

One thing should be clear—the way the independent and dependent variables are measured affects their elaboration, the specification of their relation, and the null hypothesis and statistical test. Review Table 4.4, which we developed in the previous chapter. You need to know the content to diagram the hypotheses that are examined in this chapter in order to select the appropriate statistics. See Table 4.4 for a summary of the nature of variables and the appropriate statistical test for each type.

Table 4.3 Diagram of H.1a		
Research hypothesis H.1a: *The greater the degree of hindering bureaucratic structure in schools, the greater is the sense of faculty powerlessness.*		
	Independent Variable (x)	**Dependent Variable (y)**
Name of variable:	Hindering structure	Sense of powerlessness
Kind of variable: (Continuous or categorical)	Continuous	Continuous
Elaboration of variable:	Varies from low to high	Varies from low to high
Specify relationship:	x and y vary together, or $>x$, $>y$	
Unit of analysis: (Object of study)	School	
Null hypothesis:	$r = 0$	
Statistical test to reject the null:	Correlation coefficient	

Table 4.4	Types of Variables and Appropriate Statistical Tests	
Independent Variable	Dependent Variable	Statistical Test
Dichotomous	Continuous	*t* Test
Categorical	Continuous	*F* test (ANOVA)
Categorical	Categorical	Chi-square (χ^2)
Continuous	Continuous	Correlation (*r*)
Multiple and continuous	Continuous	Multiple correlation (*R*)

Case III: Categorical Independent and Categorical Dependent Variables

Sometimes both the independent and the dependent variables are categorical. Such hypotheses are often difficult to express because it means that you need to specify the relationships between every pair of cells in the contingency table. Sociologists are most likely to develop and test hypotheses with categorical variables because their data are often reported as frequencies, often frequencies of demographic data. Generally speaking, it is wise to use continuous variables when you can because they are easier to write and talk about.

In a simple relationship in which both variables are dichotomous, expressing the relation is not too difficult. Consider the following hypothesis:

> *H.8:* Being Republican as contrasted with Democrat in the U.S. Senate leads to a conservative voting record on bills, whereas being Democrat leads to a liberal voting record.

Let's first sketch the contingency table (a 2 × 2 cross break) for the hypothesis:

	Conservative Vote	Liberal Vote
Republican		
Democrat		

What goes in each cell in the above contingency table? Frequencies—the number of people who were Republican and voted conservative, the number of Democrats who voted conservative, the number of Republicans who voted liberal, and the number of Democrats who voted liberal. If there is a relation between the two variables, then we expect that there will be disproportionate frequencies in the cells as suggested by the hypothesis.

Let's analyze and diagram the hypothesis (H.8). The independent variable is party affiliation—Republican or Democrat. The dependent variable is voting record in terms of a conservative vote or liberal vote. Both variables are categorical with two variations—hence the four cells in the contingency table. The relation is specified because Republicans are more likely to vote conservative while Democrats are more likely to vote liberal. The unit of analysis is clearly the individual; individual senators are the objects of the study. What kind of statistical test is appropriate when both variables are categorical? A chi-square (c^2) is the appropriate test for the null hypothesis. The analysis for this hypothesis is summarized in Table 4.5.

We have examined a simple case of two variables in which both were categorical with only two variations. As we suggested earlier, it gets difficult to write the hypothesis when all the variables are categorical, especially if the variables have more than two categories. Yet, you will encounter such relationships in the literature. In those cases, your statistical analysis will begin with some kind of chi-square test. Remember that measurement of the variables directly affects the kind of statistical analysis needed to test the relations. Clearly, you don't have any control over how others conceptualize and measure their variables, but if you are doing the research, try to design your measures so they are continuous, at least the dependent variable, because it simplifies things and makes your statistics more easily managed and often more powerful.

Table 4.5   Diagram of H.8

Research hypothesis H.8: Being Republican as contrasted with Democrat in the U.S. Senate leads to a conservative voting record on bills, whereas being Democrat leads to a liberal voting record.

	Independent Variable (x)	Dependent Variable (y)
Name of variable:	Party affiliation	Voting record
Kind of variable: (Continuous or categorical)	Categorical	Categorical
Elaboration of variable:	Republican (R) Democrat (D)	Conservative (C) Liberal (L)
Specify relationship:	Rs more likely to vote C and Ds more likely to vote L	
Unit of analysis: (Object of study)	Individual	
Null hypothesis:	Frequencies are the same (determined by chance)	
Statistical test to reject the null:	χ^2	

After you study Table 4.5, try diagramming the following hypothesis:

> *H.9:* Rioters are more likely to be men, whereas nonrioters are more likely to be women.

How many variables are there in this hypothesis? What kind of variables are they? What are the implications of the answers to these questions for testing the hypothesis? How likely is it that the hypothesis will be supported? Why? Can you develop a theoretical rationale to support this hypothesis?

Case IV: Categorical Independent (With More Than Two Categories) and Continuous Dependent Variables

The first case we examined was a hypothesis with a dichotomous independent variable and a continuous dependent variable (Case I). Now we extend that case by specifying an independent categorical variable with more than two categories and a continuous dependent variable. Consider the following hypothesis:

> *H.10:* College students develop greater critical thinking skills in instructor-led discussion classes than in student-led discussion classes, but students in student-led discussion classes will develop greater critical thinking skills than those in instructor lecture classes.

Using our hypothesis diagram as a guide, we ask what are the independent and dependent variables. The dependent variable, the presumed effect variable (*y*), is critical thinking skill. Critical thinking is predicted to be greater or lesser dependent on the type of classroom instruction; thus, type of classroom instruction is the presumed causal variable (*x*), the independent variable. The fact that the hypothesis states that the dependent variable (critical thinking skill) will be "greater" under different conditions of teaching suggests that the dependent variable is continuous; that is, its numerical value varies along a continuum from low to high. The independent variable is a categorical variable with three variations. We elaborate and summarize the variables a little more. The independent variable, classroom instruction, is defined and measured by three kinds of classroom instruction: teacher-led discussion, student-led discussion, and teacher lecture. The dependent variable of critical thinking skill varies in degree along a continuum from low to high: The higher the value, the greater is the critical thinking skill.

Next, we turn to the relationship—its specification, the unit of analysis, the null hypothesis, and the statistical analysis. How do we specify this relation? The key here is to make sure you understand the relation and specify it in a shorthand way. Let's use the following symbols: CT = critical thinking skill, ID = instructor-led discussion, SD = student-led discussion, and IL = instructor lecture. What does the hypothesis predict? First, the hypothesis predicts a significant difference among critical thinking in the three groups, but more than that, it specifies where the differences rest. For critical thinking skills (CT), ID > SD and SD > IL (or ID > SD > IL).

Finally, we turn to the null hypothesis, which states that there is no relationship between type of classroom instruction and critical thinking; that is, CT mean of ID = CT mean of SD = CT mean of IL. The statistical test of the null is an ANOVA because the independent variable is categorical with more than two levels and the dependent variable is continuous (review Table 4.2). The F ratio will tell us whether the results are due to chance or not. If the F ratio is significant, then we will have to use special t tests (e.g., Scheffé's unplanned comparison statistical test, or Bonferroni's multiple comparison statistical test) for the pairs of means to see which groups are significantly different. The hypothesis analysis is summarized in Table 4.6.

Table 4.6   Diagram of H.10

Research hypothesis H.10: *College students develop greater critical thinking skills in instructor-led discussion classes than in student-led discussion classes, but students in student-led discussion classes will develop greater critical thinking skills than those in instructor lecture classes.*

	Independent Variable (*x*)	Dependent Variable (*y*)
Name of variable:	Classroom instruction	Critical thinking skills
Kind of variable: (Continuous or categorical)	Categorical	Continuous
Elaboration of variable:	Instructor-led discussion (ID) Student-led discussion (SD) Instructor lecture (IL)	Varies from high to low
Specify relationship:	For critical thinking skills (CT), ID > SD and SD > IL	
Unit of analysis: (Object of study)	Individual	
Null hypothesis:	CT Mean of ID = CT Mean of SD = CT Mean of IL	
Statistical test to reject the null:	ANOVA and appropriate *t* test if *F* test is significant	

Case V: Hypotheses With More Than Two Variables

Thus far in our analyses, we have been concerned with bivariate analyses—one independent and one dependent variable. We now turn to hypotheses with more than two variables. We assess three kinds of hypotheses in this case: (1) compound hypotheses, (2) contingent hypotheses, and (3) hypotheses with multiple independent variables predicting one dependent variable. Some researchers call the latter type of hypothesis multivariate, but technically, multivariate analysis has both multiple independent and dependent variables. Suffice it to say that we do not go beyond multiple independent variables in this research primer.

Compound hypotheses. For lack of a better term, compound hypotheses are multiple, bivariate hypotheses that are combined into a single statement. Sometimes, the researcher takes a set of bivariate relations and combines them into one hypothesis, which can mislead the beginning student. Consider the following hypothesis:

> *H.11:* Relations-oriented leaders have more loyal, committed, and satisfied subordinates than do task-oriented leaders.

If you are not careful, you can be misled by this type of hypothesis. As you begin your analysis, you should quickly determine the problem. What is the independent variable? Leadership style is the independent variable, which has two variations: (1) relations oriented, and (2) task oriented. What is the dependent variable? At this point, you should begin to see the problem—there are three dependent variables in this hypothesis that have been combined in one relation. To analyze the hypothesis, it is best to separate the **compound hypothesis** into its three component relations:

> *H.11a:* Relations-oriented leaders have more loyal subordinates than do task-oriented leaders.
>
> *H.11b:* Relations-oriented leaders have more committed subordinates than do task-oriented leaders.
>
> *H.11c:* Relations-oriented leaders have more satisfied subordinates than do task-oriented leaders.

Now the analysis is simple: There are actually three hypotheses, each with an independent categorical variable and a dependent continuous variable. Analyze one, and the pattern is the same for the rest.

Contingent hypotheses. Occasionally, the researcher will find or *predict a relationship that is contingent or dependent on another variable*, a **contingent hypothesis**. Such hypotheses are more complicated, but they are also more interesting and reveal the complexity of the relation. A moderator variable (z) changes the relationship between two variables, x and y, as it changes. It is easiest to understand a moderator variable when it is categorical, but theoretically, moderator variables can be continuous or categorical. Examine the following hypothesis:

> *H.12:* When the leader has influence with superiors, task-oriented leaders have more loyal subordinates than do relations-oriented leaders, but when the leader has no influence with superiors, then relations-oriented leaders have more loyal subordinates than do task-oriented ones.

As you read this hypothesis, you should sense immediately that this is more complicated than most bivariate hypotheses. How many variables are there in this hypothesis? The answer is three—influence with superiors, loyalty, and leadership style. What are the independent and dependent variables? The independent variable is leadership style, which is categorical with two variations—task and relations oriented. The dependent variable is loyalty, which is a continuous variable ranging from low to high loyalty; the higher the numerical value, the greater is the loyalty. What about influence with superiors? You guessed it—influence is a moderator variable because it changes the relation between leadership style and loyalty; that is, the relation is contingent on the influence with superiors. Moderator variables change the relation between x and y. This hypothesis predicts that the relation between x and y will differ depending on the value of z. The hypothesis says that when we have one condition of z, we have one relation between x and y, but when we have another condition of z, we have a different relation between x and y.

Let's analyze and diagram this contingent hypothesis. We already defined the independent, dependent, and moderator variables. The independent variable and moderator variable are categorical variables, each with two variations. The dependent variable is a continuous variable. Now we need to specify the relations. When the leader has influence (I), then task-oriented leaders (TO) have more loyal (L) subordinates than do relations-oriented leaders (RO), but when the leader has no influence (NI), then relations-oriented leaders (RO) have more loyal subordinates than do task-oriented leaders (TO).

The unit of analysis is a little trickier. You might think that the unit of analysis is the individual because we are talking about leaders and followers. But, each leader is the leader of the group, and it is the loyalty of that group that we will be analyzing, and so the group is the unit of analysis. The null hypothesis is that there is no difference between the groups regardless of the value of the moderator. The statistical test here is a more complex ANOVA, which we have not explained, but which is conceptually the same idea. We summarize our analysis in Table 4.7.

Table 4.7	Diagram of H.12		
Research hypothesis H.12: *When the leader has influence with superiors, task-oriented leaders have more loyal subordinates than do relations-oriented leaders, but when the leader has no influence with superiors, then relations-oriented leaders have more loyal subordinates than do task-oriented ones.*			
	Independent Variable (x)	**Dependent Variable (y)**	**Moderator Variable (z)**
Name of variable:	Leadership style	Subordinate loyalty	Influence with superiors
Kind of variable: (Continuous or categorical)	Categorical	Continuous	Categorical
Elaboration of variable:	Task-oriented style (TO) Relations-oriented style (RO)	Varies from high to low	Influence (I) No Influence (NI)
Specify relationship:	When I, then TO > RO, but when NI, RO > TO		
Unit of analysis: (Object of study)	Group		
Null hypothesis:	Mean of TO = Mean of RO regardless of I		
Statistical test to reject the null:	Appropriate ANOVA and appropriate *F* tests		

Here is another hypothesis; you analyze and diagram it.

> *H.13:* Principals who are task oriented are more effective than principals who are relations oriented when school conditions are chaotic, but when conditions are moderately favorable, then relations oriented principals are more effective; however, when conditions are very favorable, principals who are task oriented are more effective than those who are relations oriented.

Hypotheses With Multiple Independent Variables. Sometimes researchers are interested in a set of independent variables as they relate to a single dependent variable. Suppose that the researcher is interested in predicting student achievement. Instead of only examining one independent variable, here the researcher may choose a set of independent variables to find the combined effect on the dependent variable, student achievement. Let's select a set of variables that might be relevant. The socioeconomic status (SES) of parents seems important because, in general, we expect that parents of higher SES spend more time helping their children with schoolwork, provide them with more resources, and are more supportive of academic pursuits. A second variable that seems likely to predict achievement is intelligence as measured by IQ. The motivation level of students also seems a reasonable predictor of achievement. Thus, the following hypothesis can be made:

> *H.14:* SES of parents, and intelligence and motivation of students combine to increase the level of student achievement.

This hypothesis has three independent variables—SES, intelligence, and motivation—and one dependent variable, student achievement. Without further comment, the hypothesis is analyzed in Table 4.8. Study the diagram to make sure you understand the analysis.

Note that all the variables are continuous. The statistic we are computing is a multiple coefficient of correlation, which tells us if the linear combination of the three independent variables has a significant influence on the dependent variable, student achievement. Although the hypothesis does not predict it, the regression analysis will also tell us if each of the independent variables is related to the dependent, holding constant all the other independent variables; the regression coefficient for each variable can be tested for significance by the appropriate *t* test.

THE INVISIBLE CONDITION: "OTHER THINGS BEING EQUAL"

Charters (1992) makes the important point that although most hypotheses don't state the condition, a basic assumption made in the statement of any hypothesis is that "other things are equal." In fact, he suggests that beginning researchers ought to add to their hypotheses the condition in Latin described as *ceterus paribus* or (cet. parib.), which is translated as "other things being equal." The phrase *other things* refers to

Table 4.8 Diagram of H.14

Research hypothesis H.14: Socioeconomic status (SES) of parents, and intelligence and motivation of students combine to increase the level of student achievement.

	Independent Variable (x_1)	Independent Variable (x_2)	Independent Variable (x_3)	Dependent Variable (y)
Name of variable:	SES	Intelligence	Motivation	Student achievement
Kind of variable:	Continuous	Continuous	Continuous	Continuous
Elaboration of variable:	Varies from low to high	Varies from low to high	Varies from low to high	Varies from low to high
Specify relationship:	x_1 and x_2 and x_3 combine and are positively related to y			
Unit of analysis: (Object of study)	Individual			
Null hypothesis:	$R = 0$			
Statistical test to reject the null:	Multiple regression analysis			

other relevant things. It is good to consider other variables that may be important to your hypotheses. If the researcher is aware of other variables that may be related to the dependent variable, it behooves the researcher to control for their influence. Such variables are called **control variables**; they *are variables believed to be related to the dependent variable, and if not attended to and "controlled," they might be mistaken for the effect of the independent variable.* For example, SES is a strong causal variable of student achievement, and so any study with student achievement as the dependent variable should control for SES, either statistically or in the research design. If a researcher finds that any organizational property of a school is related to student achievement, he or she must make sure that SES has been "controlled for." Otherwise, the researcher may mistakenly conclude that the variable affects school achievement when in reality the relation is spurious because it is the SES that is producing the significant relation, not the independent variable.

SUMMARY

The purpose of this chapter was to examine the nature and meaning of hypotheses; the following propositions summarize the major ideas:

- A hypothesis is a conjectural statement that suggests the relationship between two or more variables.

- A good hypothesis is declarative, clear, has at least two variables, and must be amenable to testing.

- A substantive hypothesis is a declarative statement that describes the relation between the concepts—it is theoretical. Strong substantive hypotheses evolve from sound theory and are explicit in predicting the direction of the relation.

- Substantive hypotheses, however, must be transformed into statistical hypotheses to be tested.

- There are two kinds of statistical hypotheses: the null and the alternative.

- A null hypothesis is a statement that indicates that there is no relation between the measures of the variable, whereas the alternative hypothesis specifies the relation between the measures of the variables.

- Simply put, the idea is to reject the null and accept the directed alternative hypothesis.

- There are many declarative statements that masquerade as hypotheses, but in reality they are often imposters, tautologies, or misconceived, incomplete, or untestable relations.

- We have proposed a scheme for diagramming and critiquing hypotheses that ferrets out the imposters. The diagramming scheme has six steps:

1. *Identify* the independent, dependent, and moderating variables.

2. *Determine* the nature of each variable (categorical or continuous).

3. *Elaborate* each variable (What does the number mean?).

4. *Specify* the relation.

5. *Decide* on the unit of analysis.

6. *Determine* the appropriate statistical test for the null.

CHECK YOUR UNDERSTANDING

Below are a series of hypotheses. Carefully analyze and diagram each one.

H.1: Teachers who are not people oriented are more likely to leave teaching than those who are people oriented, whereas teachers who are people oriented are more likely to stay than those who are not people oriented.

H.2: Elementary schools have a greater degree of self-regulatory climate than secondary schools.

H.3: Task-oriented leaders are more effective than relations-oriented leaders when the group is cohesive, but relations-oriented leaders are more effective than task-oriented leaders when the group is noncohesive.

H.4: The greater the degree of self-regulatory climate, the higher the level of achievement of students.

H.5: The greater a parent's sense of powerlessness in school affairs, the stronger is the parent's opposition to the school district budget referenda.

H.6: Organic school bureaucracies have more open organizational climates than do enabling ones, but enabling bureaucracies are more open in climate than are mechanistic ones, and mechanistic bureaucracies are more open in climate than are autocratic ones.

H.7: Democratic supervisors have teachers who demonstrate more creativity and enthusiasm in teaching than those teachers who have autocratic supervisors.

H.8: The greater the size of a community college's instructional faculty, the greater the degree of centralization in their decision making.

H.9: Principals are more humanistic in their pupil control orientation than are their faculties.

H.10: The greater the academic optimism of a school's culture, the greater the degree of self-regulation.

H.11: Schools with high levels of trust in parents have higher school achievement levels than schools with low levels of trust in parents.

H.12: In urban schools, custodial pupil control is positively related to student achievement, but in suburban schools, custodial pupil control is negatively related to student achievement.

H.13: Teachers who have high academic optimism have higher levels of classroom student achievement than teachers with low academic optimism.

H.14: In urban schools, task-oriented teachers are more effective than relations-oriented teachers, but in suburban schools, relations-oriented teachers are more effective than task-oriented teachers.

H.15: The more diversity on the board of education, the more comprehensive is the curriculum of the school district.

H.16: Democratic senators are more likely to vote liberal, whereas Republican senators are more likely to vote conservative.

KEY TERMS

5

GENERATING HYPOTHESES

In the previous chapter, we focused our attention on finding and analyzing hypotheses. In this chapter, we are concerned with generating hypotheses. Now, we should know a good hypothesis when we see one, but how do we develop our own original hypotheses? What is the role of theory in hypothesis development? Where do people get their ideas for good hypotheses? How do we ensure that our hypotheses make good sense? Are any hypotheses really original? What are appropriate hypotheses for a doctoral dissertation? These are the kinds of questions we tackle in this chapter. Development of hypotheses is the creative part of science; it is your opportunity to play with ideas, concepts, and theories and synthesize your thinking.

IDEAS FOR NEW HYPOTHESES

Where does one get ideas for new hypotheses? There is no single answer to the question. Some people are careful observers; they note patterns of behavior in situations and speculate about why these patterns appear. They ask what the crucial concepts are that capture the essence of their observations. In other words, they conceptualize their observations as they begin to think abstractly about what they are seeing. They link their concepts with other concepts as they develop explanations (theories). Others read good research journals in related fields and begin to wonder if the findings apply to schools. Do these results in business organizations apply to schools? Do I need to replicate this study with teachers, administrators, and schools? Still others find themselves engaged by a new theoretical framework. Does the underlying theory hold in schools? Does this theory apply to teachers and school administrators? Perhaps a good way to illustrate each of these paths to new hypotheses is with specific examples.

OBSERVING, CONCEPTUALIZING, AND HYPOTHESIZING

When I was a beginning doctoral student, my advisor got me involved with a team organized to study schools. The first phase of the broad study was an exploratory investigation of a single school in Pennsylvania. For more than a year, a team of researchers composed of students and professors made trips to a junior high school to observe what was happening. During the year, the team of researchers did a comprehensive case study of the school—spending hundreds of hours observing and recording student-teacher, teacher-teacher, and administrator-teacher interactions in places of high visibility, such as the faculty lounge, faculty meetings, assemblies, and the cafeteria. Pupil control was the dominant motif and integrative theme that gave meaning to much of what was happening in the school. Indeed, we were struck by the saliency of pupil control, a fact that was vividly demonstrated by a host of examples:

- The widespread suspicion of teachers that the guidance counselors were undermining their authority when they dealt with students

- The fear that the new principal would be weak on discipline

- The continuous, and often emotional, discussions about student discipline in the faculty lounge

- The cafeteria and assembly halls serving as "proving grounds" for new teachers to demonstrate that they could "handle" difficult students

- The single roll of toilet paper padlocked and chained to the wall in the boys' lavatory—a symbol of the coercive control that pervaded the school

These observations led to a series of questions (see "Elements of a Proposal," Appendix A). Why was pupil control so important? How should we conceptualize pupil control? What causes teachers and administrators to be so concerned with control? To what extent is what we observed in this school common in other schools? Is such concern for control as pervasive in other kinds of organizations? If so, what kinds of organizations?

SEARCHING FOR
THEORETICAL UNDERPINNINGS

To answer these and other questions, we did some conceptualizing and theorizing. Let me give you a sense of the conceptual framework we ultimately developed to answer the questions. We found that Richard Carlson's (1964) theoretical analysis of service organizations was especially useful in explaining why control was so salient in schools. Schools, like prisons and public mental hospitals, are service organizations in which *clients have no say in their participation*—they must participate—and the *organizations have no choice in selecting clients*—they must take them all. It is not surprising that in service organizations with mandatory participation and unselected clients, some participants do not want to take advantage of the services offered by the organization; hence, control is a problem. To be sure, there are dramatic differences among prisons, public mental hospitals, and schools, but the mandatory participation and unselected clients in these service organizations inevitably ensure that client control is the central aspect of organizational life.

The next challenge was to conceptualize pupil control. A number of frameworks were considered: Etzioni's (1962) notion of coercive and normative control; Lewin, Lippitt, and White's (1939) framework of authoritarian and democratic control; and Rotter's (1954) theory of internal and external locus of control, among others. Eventually, we settled on the work of Gilbert and Levinson (1957) based on their study of patients in public mental hospitals. They conceptualized client control as being along a continuum of custodial to humanistic, and so did we. There were two compelling reasons for selecting their framework over the others. First, a custodial approach was theoretically consistent with the problems of control of unselected clients in service organizations. Second, the framework was a good fit with the extant theory of teaching and learning; that is, humanistic pupil control was consistent with the discovery method of teaching and learning and other educational reforms popular in the 1960s. Even today, a humanistic perspective on pupil control fits current constructivist approaches (Hoy & Miskel, 2008). We conceived pupil control as being along a continuum from a **custodial orientation** at one pole to a humanistic perspective at the other extreme.

The model for the custodial orientation is the traditional school, where behavior is rigid and tightly controlled; order is a primary concern. Students are stereotyped in terms of their appearance, behavior, and parents' social status. Teachers with a custodial orientation to pupil control see students as irresponsible and undisciplined individuals who must be controlled by punitive and coercive action.

Teachers do not attempt to understand student behavior. They view misbehavior in moralistic terms and as a personal affront. School is an autocratic organization with strict status distinctions between teachers and students. Students must accept the decisions of teachers without question. The flow of power and communication is unilateral and downward, and cynicism, impersonality, and watchful mistrust imbue the custodial orientation.

The model for the **humanistic orientation** is the school as a learning community, where individuals learn by cooperative interaction and experience. Interpersonal relationships are warm and friendly. Behaviors are interpreted in psychological and sociological terms, not moralistic ones. Self-discipline and self-regulation are goals that are substituted for rigid and strict teacher control. Teachers see the school as a democratic organization with two-way communication between students and teachers and increased self-determination of students. A humanistic orientation is marked by optimism, openness, flexibility, understanding, and increased student self-determination. Both teachers and students are willing to act on their own volition and then accept responsibility for their actions.

Theoretical Assumptions

One general assumption of our work was that both social and psychological factors influenced the attitudes and behaviors of educators; thus, we were concerned about both role and personality factors in any explanation of patterns of pupil control in schools.

Another assumption of our work was that much of what happens in schools is a function of attempts of individuals to maintain and enhance their status relative to others. We assumed that when status is threatened, the natural tendency is for individuals to protect themselves by adopting a stance that they believe helps them control the threat. For example, there is ample evidence of teachers who try to maintain their status relative to students. Just consider the dress of teachers (shirt and tie) and the mode of address ("Mr." or "Ms."), as well as the use of punishment, such as detention, verbal reprimands, and sending unruly students to the office. These are common behaviors used by teachers to maintain and enhance their status.

Finally, the status of teachers and principals is grounded in the nature of the school and in the requirements of the role. That is, many status problems for public school educators are accentuated by the fact that schools are service organizations with mandatory participation and unselected clients. Teachers in particular are affected by the requirement that they deal directly with these unselected student clients, many of whom do not want to be in school. We postulated that when the status of educators is threatened, they turn to custodial means to gain control over the situation.

Developing Theoretical Rationales and Generating Hypotheses

The theoretical arguments we developed led to the first set of hypotheses. See both "Elements of Proposal" (Appendix A) and "A Few Writing Tips" (Appendix B) for further suggestions about developing and stating your ideas. We first considered role factors that would enhance or reduce the threat to the status of teachers, administrators, and guidance counselors. We assumed that elementary students, compared with secondary students, pose less of a threat to teacher status. We reasoned that smaller, younger, and less mature elementary students pose neither the physical nor the intellectual threat as that of their larger, older, and more mature counterparts. Some secondary students are larger and smarter than their teachers. Furthermore, adolescents also are moving toward identification with peers, not adults. They are apprehensive about how they are viewed by their peers and are more concerned with saving face with peers than with either parents or teachers. If our theory is correct, then the following two hypotheses are logical:

> *H.1:* Secondary teachers are more custodial in their pupil control ideology than are elementary teachers.

> *H.2:* Secondary principals should be more custodial in pupil control ideology than should elementary principals.

What about teachers compared with principals? Here, we assumed that those individuals who had to deal directly with unselected student clients would be more threatened and thus more custodial in their pupil control ideology. When a student misbehaves in the classroom, the teacher is on stage: All the students are watching to see what the teacher will do. Typically, teachers don't disappoint—they perform. They act angry. They show who is in charge. Their response is often to punish those who have the audacity to challenge them. A quick response is required. On the other hand, the principal usually sees an unruly student in the privacy of the office. The privacy in itself makes the interaction less threatening, and the situation is more conducive to an analysis of the causes of the misbehavior. Contrary to the commonsense notion that the principal is in charge and needs to demonstrate his or her authority, our theory suggests that the principal's status is less threatened by the students than is the teacher's status; hence, we hypothesized as follows:

> *H.3:* Teachers are more custodial in their pupil control ideology than are their principals.

Using the notion of "threat to status" as a cause for custodial behavior, we predicted the following:

H.4: Teachers are more custodial in pupil control ideology than are guidance counselors.

Teachers learn the appropriate roles for teaching through the socialization process. They are socialized to the requisite roles and behavior both formally and informally, that is, through education and experience. New teachers receive much of their initial socialization to teaching in their preparation programs, which are for the most part idealistic and humanistic (Hoy, 1967, 1968, 1969; Hoy & Woolfolk, 1990). Experience is also a strong socialization agent; in fact, we assumed that the most significant socialization takes place on the job, especially during the first year. Evidence from a number of studies consistently demonstrates that the teacher subculture in public schools tends to be custodial (Coleman, 1961; Hoy & Woolfolk, 1990; Waller, 1932; Willower & Jones, 1967). Good teaching is often equated with good control. Hence, we predicted the following:

H.5: Experienced teachers are more custodial in their pupil control ideology than are beginning teachers.

In addition to how social and role factors influenced pupil control ideology, we were interested in the impact of personality. Beginning with the classic studies on fascism of Adorno, Brunswick, Levinson, and Sanford (1950), the authoritarian personality has been a major focus of study for many years, but it remains a puzzle to contemporary social scientists (Altemeyer, 1996). In the early studies (Adorno et al., 1950), authoritarianism was conceived of as a right-wing affliction, but others have viewed it as a personality characteristic that varies across the spectrum of political and religious beliefs (Altemeyer, 1996; Rokeach, 1960).

The underlying theory of the authoritarian personality suggests that custodial control is a facet of the authoritarian personality; indeed, Gilbert and Levinson (1957) demonstrated the truth of that proposition in their study of public mental hospitals. We were concerned with a more general notion of authoritarianism that was unrelated to political ideology. To that end, we selected Rokeach's (1960) framework of **dogmatism**, which refers to the structure of one's beliefs rather than the content of the beliefs. Dogmatism *is the structure of one's belief system; it deals with how one believes rather than with what one believes.* Dogmatism is a general notion of authoritarianism conceptualized along a continuum from closed-mindedness (authoritarian) to open-mindedness (nonauthoritarian). We assumed that those who have a personality disposition toward authoritarianism, that is, who want things concrete, who disdain ambiguity, and who revere authority, would also embrace custodial control; hence, we predicted as follows:

H.6: Regardless of role or school level, closed-minded educators are more custodial in their pupil control ideology than open-minded ones.

Our continued effort to understand the relationship between teaching practice and student behavior led us to Deci and Ryan's (1985, 2000, 2008) formulation of Self-Determination Theory (SDT). The five major underlying assumptions of the theory are:

1. All individuals have the potential for adaptation and growth.

2. Growth behaviors are driven by autonomous, self-determined motivation.

3. Autonomous motivation emerges from social conditions that fulfill the basic psychological needs of autonomy, competence, and relatedness.

4. Adaptation and growth are undermined by controlling social environments.

5. Individuals thrive and prosper when experiences and tasks nurture their basic psychological needs for autonomy, competence, and relatedness.

Like all individuals, students are driven by three important needs: the needs of autonomy, competence, and relatedness. In particular, evidence demonstrates that teachers who support student needs of autonomy and competence facilitate student identification with school (Chirkov & Ryan, 2001; Reeve, 2002), build self-esteem (Deci, Vallerand, Pelletier, & Ryan, 1991), and increase interest in schoolwork (Tsai, Kunter, Ludtke, Trautwein, & Ryan, 2008). Further, controlling instructional practices undermine student interest in learning (Tsai et al., 2008) and thwart autonomy (Reeve, 2002). Thus, we expect that student autonomy leads to increased levels of engagement, and the following hypothesis is proposed:

> H.7: The greater the degree of teacher support for student autonomy, the greater the extent of student engagement.

Let's review. We started with the notion of the importance of pupil control in schools, which grew from our observations of behaviors in one school and our analysis of the school as a service organization with mandatory participation and unselected clients. Then, we conceptualized pupil control in terms of ideology along a continuum from custodial to humanistic. Next, we developed some theoretical underpinnings for explanations of what role and personality variables were related to pupil control and why. We used SDT to explain further how student behavior is a function of the interaction of the external environment and psychological needs. Finally, we used our theoretical assumptions to elaborate theoretical rationales for each hypothesis as we generated a set of seven hypotheses. These hypotheses were clearly and concisely stated.

MORE THEORY: MORE HYPOTHESES

We now turn to social cognitive theory to generate a series of hypotheses on self-efficacy. Albert Bandura's (1977, 1986, 1997) social cognitive theory is a comprehensive psychological perspective that explains aspects of individual behavior. The general assumption of the theory is that thought, action, and emotion are a function of the interaction of behavior, personal factors, and environmental forces; moreover, behavior, personal factors, and external environment reciprocally cause each other; that is, the pairs of variables both cause and affect each other.

Self-Efficacy

One key component of the social cognitive perspective is self-efficacy theory. Self-efficacy is an individual's belief that he or she has the capacity to organize and execute the behavior in order to be successful in a particular situation. To illustrate the utility of this concept, we examine a few of the assumptions of self-efficacy theory:

- Individuals develop beliefs or judgments about their cognitive, social, and behavioral competencies through mastery learning—successful experiences in a specific area of concern.

- Individuals cultivate beliefs in their capabilities to use their talents wisely.

- Judgments of personal efficacy affect one's goals and choice of action.

- Beliefs about self-efficacy determine the level of motivation; the higher the degree of self-efficacy in a particular situation, the stronger the motivation.

- Although mastery experiences are most important in developing self-efficacy, vicarious experience, persuasion, and physiological states are also sources of self-efficacy.

- Individuals have the capacity for self-direction, self-motivation, and self-regulation.

Next, let's examine a few key assumptions of goal theory.

- Individuals are motivated by goals.

- Specific goals are more effective than general ones.

- To be effective, goals must also be realistic and challenging.

- To be effective, the individual must embrace the goals.

- Goals are effective because they focus attention, mobilize effort, and enhance persistence.

- The combined influence of goals and feedback on performance regulates and heightens motivation.

- Goal accomplishment positively influences self-efficacy, and self-efficacy reinforces the setting of realistic goals.

To be sure, we have simplified both self-efficacy theory and goal theory, but these assumptions will serve as bases for developing a set of hypotheses. In social cognitive theory (Bandura, 1986, 1997), self-regulation of motivation and performance attainment is governed by a number of self-regulatory mechanisms that operate simultaneously. Personal self-efficacy is one of the mechanisms that has a central role in the regulatory process. There is a difference between having competencies and skills and being able to use them well in difficult situations. To be successful, one must have not only the required skills, but also a persistent and resilient belief in one's capacity to exercise control over situations in order to accomplish the desired goals and objectives. Thus, it seems reasonable to assume that individuals with the same skills may perform well or poorly depending on whether their self-beliefs enhance or impair their motivation and problem solving (Wood & Bandura, 1989).

What kinds of self-beliefs enhance motivation and problem solving? From the work of Wood and Bandura (1989), we propose that an individual's belief about whether cognitive ability is a fixed or an acquired skill is important. When confronted with a difficult problem, it is reasonable to assume that individuals who believe that they can improve their ability, compared with those who believe that their ability is fixed, will have higher levels of self-efficacy as well as perform at higher levels. Hence, we propose the following hypotheses:

> *H.8:* School administrators who believe that their cognitive capacity is an acquired skill have higher levels of self-efficacy than do those who believe that cognitive capacity is fixed.

> *H.9:* School administrators who believe that their cognitive ability is an acquired skill set more challenging goals for themselves than do those who believe that their cognitive capacity is fixed.

H.10: School administrators who believe that their cognitive ability is an acquired skill use analytic strategies more effectively than do those who believe that their cognitive capacity is fixed.

Another important self-belief is one's ability to control the environment or work situation. Again, it seems reasonable to propose that when individuals believe that they have control over key aspects of the environment, then they are motivated to exercise personal efficacy, which enhances the likelihood of success. Thus, consider the following hypotheses:

H.11: School administrators who believe that the environment is controllable have higher levels of self-efficacy than do administrators who believe that the environment is not controllable.

H.12: School administrators who believe that the environment is controllable have higher levels of job performance than do administrators who believe that the environment is not controllable.

H.13: School administrators who believe that the environment is controllable set more and more difficult goals than do administrators who believe that the environment is not controllable.

Finally, let's examine the type of goal and motivation. Goal theory suggests that specific goals are more effective motivators than are general ones. Hence, one would expect that the admonition to "do your best" is less effective than a specific, challenging goal.

H.14: School administrators who are challenged with a realistic, specific goal are more highly motivated than are those who simply face the general goal of "do your best."

H.15: School administrators who are challenged with a realistic, specific goal perform at higher levels than do those who simply face the general goal of "do your best."

Using social cognitive theory, self-efficacy theory, goal theory, and previous research, the last eight hypotheses were generated. With a little more reading and study of the research and theoretical literature, we could continue to develop additional hypotheses linking self-efficacy, motivation, performance, and achievement.

The theories are appropriate for generating hypotheses not only about school administrators, but also about teachers and students. Thus far, we have generated individual hypotheses. Sometimes, the set of hypotheses can be developed into a more complex set of relations called causal models. For example, Wood and Bandura (1989) use many of the hypotheses above to generate a causal model relating mastery experience, personal goals, self-efficacy, analytic strategy, and performance. Examine the model in Figure 5.1, in which we predict the causal connections among many of the variables and hypotheses for beginning school administrators. Mastery experience in the form of successful experience leads to both personal goals and self-efficacy beliefs; self-efficacy influences action strategies, which in turn, along with personal goals, influence the performance of school administrators.

Collective Efficacy

One of the challenges for those who study schools is to learn how school organizations can contribute to students' academic success. Indeed, it has been difficult to find school characteristics that influence student achievement if the socioeconomic status (SES) of the school is controlled. Bandura (1993, 1997) argues that one powerful construct that varies greatly among schools and that is systematically associated with student achievement is the collective efficacy of teachers within a school. We just examined self-efficacy as a concept that is likely related to individual success at specific tasks, including teaching. In this section, we extend the notion of self-efficacy to the collective level, that is, the collective efficacy of the school.

Collective efficacy, *the perceptions of teachers in a school that the efforts of the faculty as a whole will have a positive effect on students*, is based on Bandura's (1977, 1986, 1997) social cognitive theory and is concerned with human agency, or the ways in which people exercise some level of control over their own lives. Central to the exercise of control is a sense of self-efficacy, or "beliefs in one's capabilities to organize and execute a course of action required to produce a given attainment" (Bandura, 1997, p. 3). But, social cognitive theory acknowledges that "personal agency operates within a broad network of sociostructural influences" (p. 6), and thus, the theory "extends the analysis of mechanisms of human agency to the exercise of collective agency" (p. 7)—people's shared beliefs that they can work together to produce effects.

Teachers' shared beliefs influence the social milieu of schools (Hoy & Miskel, 2008). Within an organization, perceived collective efficacy represents the shared perceptions of group members concerning "the performance capability of a social system as a whole" (Bandura, 1997, p. 469). Analogous to self-efficacy, collective efficacy is associated with the tasks, level of effort, persistence, shared thoughts, stress levels, and achievement of groups.

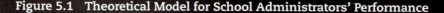

Figure 5.1 Theoretical Model for School Administrators' Performance

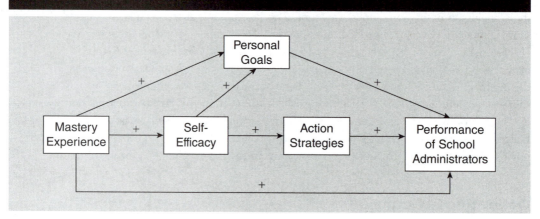

According to Bandura (1993, 1997), collective teacher efficacy is an important school property. One reason for this conclusion is the link between teacher efficacy and student achievement (Ashton & Webb, 1986; Ross, 1992, 1998). Just as individual teacher efficacy may partially explain the effect of teachers on student achievement, from an organizational perspective, collective teacher efficacy can explain the differential effect that schools have on student achievement. Collective teacher efficacy, therefore, has the potential to contribute to our understanding of how schools differ in the attainment of their most important objective—the education of students.

Bandura (1997) observes that because schools present teachers with a host of unique challenges involving concepts, such as public accountability, shared responsibility for student outcomes, and minimal control over work environments, the task of developing high levels of collective teacher efficacy is difficult, but not impossible. Moreover, there is reason to believe that collective teacher efficacy, once developed, will thrive. At the collective level, efficacy beliefs are social perceptions. Putnam (1993) refers to such social features as moral resources—ones that are strengthened rather than depleted through their use. The potential for efficacy to grow rather than deplete through use is also indicated by the cyclic nature of efficacy implied by reciprocal causality (Bandura, 1997).

Because social cognitive theory specifies that teachers' perceptions of self and group capability influence their actions, it follows that these actions will be judged by the group relative to group norms, such as those set by collective efficacy beliefs. According to Coleman (1985, 1987), norms develop to permit group members some control over the actions of others when those actions have consequences for the group. When a teacher's actions are incongruent with the shared beliefs of the group, the teacher's actions will be sanctioned by group members; in fact, Coleman argues that the severity of the social sanctions delivered to those who break norms will be equal in magnitude to the effect of norm breaking on the collective. Thus, if most teachers in a school are highly efficacious, the normative environment will press teachers to persist in their educational efforts. Moreover, the press to perform will be accompanied by social sanctions for those who do not.

Collective teacher efficacy beliefs shape the normative environment of a school; hence, they have a strong influence over teacher behavior, and consequently student achievement. When collective efficacy is high, teachers in a school believe that they can reach their students and overcome negative external influences. Given these beliefs, teachers are more persistent in their efforts; they plan more, they accept responsibility for student achievement, and temporary setbacks or failures do not discourage them. Strong collective efficacy perceptions not only enhance individual teacher performance, but also influence the pattern of shared beliefs held by organizational members. The influence of group norms constrains a teacher with average personal efficacy beliefs to exert even more effort on joining a faculty with high levels of collective teacher efficacy. We theorize that such behavioral changes reflect the normative effect of a school's collective efficacy on its individual members (Goddard, Hoy, & Woolfolk Hoy, 2004). Thus, we predict the following:

> *H.16:* The greater the collective efficacy of a school, the higher is the level of student achievement at the school level.

> *H.17:* The greater the collective efficacy of a school, the greater is the individual sense of teacher efficacy.

In the same vein, we would expect the self-efficacy of the principal to be related to the self-efficacy of the teacher and collective efficacy of the school. Consider the following hypotheses:

> *H.18:* The greater the collective efficacy of the principal, the greater is the individual sense of teacher efficacy.

> *H.19:* The greater the collective efficacy of the principal, the greater is the collective efficacy of the school.

What other factors produce schools with a strong sense of collective efficacy? Note that the preceding question is a research problem. We have already suggested that the self-efficacy of the principal is likely related to the collective efficacy of the school (H.18). There are probably many variables that enhance the collective efficacy of the school. Consider, for example, the transformational leadership of the principal (Leithwood,

1994), participative school decision-making structures (Hoy & Tarter, 2008), principal authenticity (Henderson & Hoy, 1982), the mindfulness of the principal (Hoy, 2003), and the structure of the school (Hoy & Sweetland, 2000), just to mention a few likely candidates. *Frame a few hypotheses using these concepts.* As an example of generating another theory-based hypothesis, let's focus on the structure of the school.

Enabling structure is a construct that denotes the effectiveness of structures and processes in aiding the work of teachers. Specifically, *enabling structure captures teachers' beliefs about how well the school as an organization works in supporting the teaching task.* A connection between enabling structures and collective efficacy is easy to imagine. The link can be framed around Bandura's (1997) four sources of efficacy beliefs—mastery experience, vicarious experience, social persuasion, and affective state.

The school structure provides significant opportunities for increasing mastery experiences. When a school makes time or resources available to improve teachers' instructional methods, it is increasing the opportunities for successful teaching and thus for mastery experiences. On a more practical level, skillful principals take advantage of school structures to place teachers in assignments where they can undergo mastery experiences rather than be overwhelmed or bored. Similarly, organizational structures and processes, such as providing relevant professional development, using master teachers, finding ways to allow teachers to observe other teachers' classroom practices, and developing processes that encourage teachers' group discussion and reflection on their work all provide opportunities for both vicarious experiences (modeling) and verbal persuasion. Finally, the affective states of teachers are likely to be significantly influenced by their perceptions of whether the school organization enables rather than hinders their work (McGuigan & Hoy, 2006).

Because the principal heavily influences school organizational structures, policies, procedures, and rules, enabling bureaucracy may serve as a proxy for aspects of capable leadership. Elsewhere, we have stressed the importance of school leadership in determining whether a school bureaucracy is enabling or hindering (Hoy, 2003; Hoy & Sweetland, 2000). Although it is neither a direct measure of leadership traits nor style, enabling structure is a product of leader actions and an indirect way to influence collective efficacy. Enabling bureaucracy may capture the outcomes of what effective leaders actually do—enable the key work of the school. Thus, the following hypotheses are proposed:

> *H.20:* The more enabling the structure of the school, the greater is the collective efficacy of the school.

> *H.21:* The more enabling the structure of the school, the greater is the individual teacher sense of efficacy.

H.22: Enabling school structure works indirectly through the collective efficacy of the school to improve school achievement.

Although we have been developing hypotheses with only two variables, many of these relationships can be connected and examined simultaneously. That is, a causal model can be developed and tested using multivariate techniques. Causal models are complex and deal with multiple variables. We illustrated such a model in Figure 5.1; now, we turn to another model relating structure, collective efficacy, teacher efficacy, and school achievement while controlling for a number of other variables that are related to student achievement, such as the socioeconomic level of the school, prior achievement, and urbanicity. Examine Figure 5.2, and note how these variables relate to each other and how the model represents an entire set of hypotheses.

Academic Optimism

We conclude this chapter by examining the concept of academic optimism, which is a collective property of schools, and we develop our final set of hypotheses. Unlike the other concepts in this chapter, academic optimism is a latent construct; that is, it comprises three more basic concepts—collective efficacy, academic emphasis of the school, and faculty trust in students and parents. To understand the construct, we must first look at each of its components and how they come together to form an integrated whole.

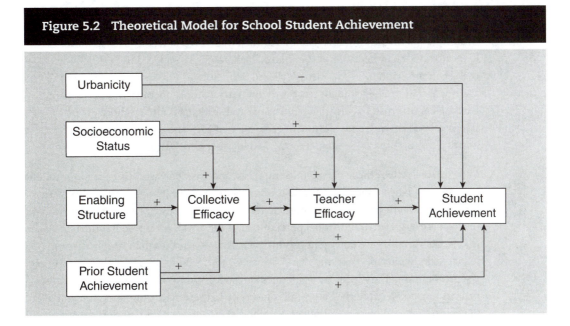

Figure 5.2 Theoretical Model for School Student Achievement

Collective efficacy has been conceptualized and defined in the previous section as the perceptions of teachers in a school that the efforts of the faculty as a whole will have a positive effect on students. Some of the hypotheses generated above relating collective efficacy with school student achievement have been supported by and support Bandura's social cognitive and self-efficacy theory (Goddard, Hoy et al., 2004; Goddard, LoGerfo, & Hoy, 2004).

Academic emphasis is *the extent to which the school is driven by a quest for academic excellence—a press for academic achievement.* High, but achievable academic goals are set for students; the learning environment is orderly and serious; students are motivated to work hard; and students respect academic achievement (Hoy & Miskel, 2008; Hoy, Tarter, & Kottkamp, 1991). Academic emphasis is another one of the few school variables directly related to school achievement; in fact, whether school effectiveness is conceived of as the commitment of teachers to the school, the teachers' judgments of the effectiveness of the school, or actual school test scores, academic emphasis makes a significant positive difference, even controlling for SES and regardless of school level—elementary, middle, or secondary (Goddard, Sweetland, & Hoy, 2000; Hoy et al., 1991; Hoy & Hannum, 1997; Hoy & Sabo, 1998; Hoy, Tarter, & Bliss, 1990; Lee & Bryk, 1989).

Faculty trust in parents and students—the faculty's willingness to be vulnerable and work with parents and students based on the confidence that parents and students are serious partners who are benevolent, reliable, competent, honest, and open—is also a collective school property, in the same fashion as collective efficacy and academic emphasis. Surprisingly, trust in parents and trust in students is a unitary concept. Although one might think that the two are separate, several factor analyses have demonstrated that they are not (Goddard, Tschannen-Moran, & Hoy, 2001; Hoy & Tschannen-Moran, 1999). Also, Bryk and Schneider (2002) make the theoretical argument that teacher-student trust in elementary schools operates primarily through teacher-parent trust. Faculty trust in parents and students is also a school property that is related to student achievement regardless of SES and other demographic characteristics (Bryk & Schneider, 2002; Goddard et al., 2001; Hoy, 2002).

Why are collective efficacy, academic emphasis, and trust consistently related to student achievement when controlling for SES whereas most other school-level qualities are not? Is there some common and more general theoretical base for these properties? All of them are aggregated individual perceptions of the *group*, as opposed to the *individual*; that is, the variables are emergent group-level attributes rather than simply the sum of teachers' individual perceptions (Bandura, 1986, 1997). The three concepts have much else in common: They focus on academics and success, they are positive and optimistic in their perspective, and they are similar not only in their nature and function, but also in their potent and positive influence on schools; in fact, we have demonstrated that the three collective properties work together in a unified fashion to create a positive academic environment that we call *school academic optimism* (Hoy, Tarter, & Woolfolk Hoy, 2006b).

Many conceptions treat optimism as a cognitive characteristic—a goal or expectancy based on knowledge and thinking (Peterson, 2000; Snyder et al., 2002). Our conception of academic optimism includes both cognitive and affective (emotional) dimensions and adds a behavioral element. Collective efficacy is a group belief that reflects the thoughts and expectations of the group; it is *cognitive*. Faculty trust in parents and students is an *affective* response. Academic emphasis is the press for particular *behaviors* in the school workplace; it captures the behavioral enactment of efficacy and trust (Hoy et al., 2006b). In brief, academic optimism paints a rich picture of human agency that explains collective behavior in terms of cognitive, affective, and behavioral dimensions.

The relationships between the three major dimensions of academic optimism have been graphically presented as a triadic set of interactions with each element functionally dependent on the others. Faculty trust in parents and students encourages a sense of collective efficacy, and collective efficacy reinforces and enhances the trust. Similarly, when the faculty trusts parents, teachers can insist on higher academic standards with the confidence that they will not be undermined by parents, and high academic standards in turn reinforce the faculty trust. Finally, when the faculty believes that it has the capability to organize and execute actions for a positive effect on student achievement, it emphasizes academic achievement, and academic emphasis in turn reinforces a strong sense of collective efficacy. In sum, all the elements of academic optimism are in transactional relationships with each other and interact to create a culture of academic optimism in the school. This postulated reciprocal causality between each pair of elements is shown in Figure 5.3.

We chose to call this overarching construct academic optimism because it unites efficacy, trust, and academic emphasis with a sense of the possible. Let's review. Efficacy is the belief that the faculty can make a positive contribution to student learning: *The faculty believes that it can make a difference*. Faculty trust is the belief that teachers, parents, and students can cooperate to improve learning: *Students can learn*. Academic emphasis is the enacted behavior prompted by these beliefs; that is, *the faculty can press for achievement*. Thus, a school with high academic optimism is a collectivity in which the faculty believes that *it can* make a difference, that *students can* learn, and that academic performance *can be* achieved. Another attraction to the term *academic optimism* is the idea that optimism can be learned; a pessimistic school can become optimistic. Administrators and teachers have reason to be optimistic. They can be empowered; neither they nor their students are irretrievably trapped by social conditions.

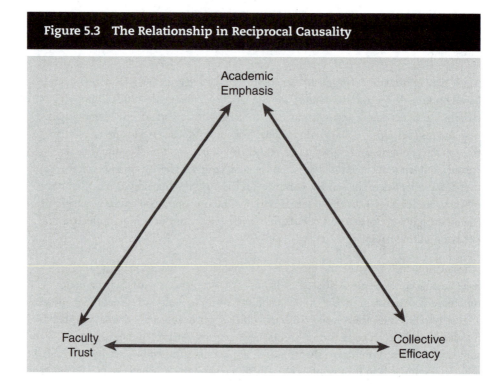

Figure 5.3   The Relationship in Reciprocal Causality

This preceding theoretical analysis led to two more hypotheses (Hoy et al., 2006b). We go beyond the nature of academic optimism as we propose a test of the academic optimism/achievement relationship:

> *H.23:* The academic achievement of a school is a function of academic optimism, controlling for SES, population density, and previous student achievement.

Furthermore, we expected that SES and previous achievement were directly related to both academic optimism and student achievement, but that both also made indirect contributions to achievement through academic optimism. Hence, we hypothesized as follows:

> *H.24:* SES and previous student achievement make direct contributions to the academic achievement of a school as well as indirect contributions to achievement through academic optimism.

Both of these hypotheses are illustrated in the path model in Figure 5.4 and can be tested simultaneously using more sophisticated regression analysis techniques, which we have not discussed in this text (Hoy et al., 2006b).

Figure 5.4 Theoretical Path Model of Academic Optimism and School Achievement

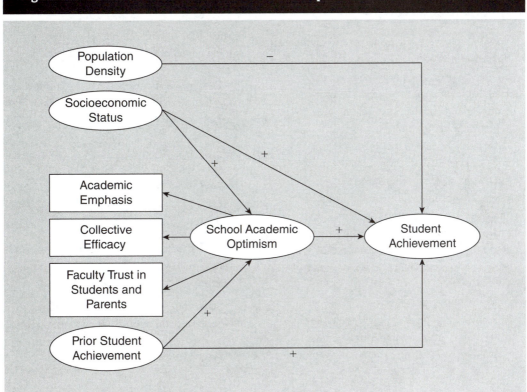

SUMMARY

- The previous chapter focused on identifying and critiquing hypotheses, while this chapter explores the generation of original, testable hypotheses that are anchored in strong theory. The purpose is to illustrate the process of developing hypotheses. We generated almost two dozen hypotheses in this chapter.

- Most of these ideas come from our own thinking and research. Some are more original than others, but all of them push our understanding a little further of important facets of schools, administration, and teaching.

- An inventive mind is indispensable to developing hypotheses. Learn to play with concepts and ideas, and stretch the concepts you like.

- For example, we just introduced and discussed the academic optimism of schools, which is clearly a collective property of schools. You may be more interested in the academic optimism of principals or teachers or even students. Apply the construct to individuals. Does it make sense? Does it have the same dimensions? Just think of how many interesting new hypotheses you can generate using the academic optimism of principals and academic optimism of teachers as they relate to teaching, learning, organization, communication, decision making, leadership, school politics, and on and on. Give it a try!

- In generating hypotheses, there is no substitute for good theory, just as there is no proxy for an inventive mind. Even if your initial idea comes from careful observation of

events, in the end, finding a sound theoretical perspective will enhance and enrich your hypotheses.

- Clearly there can be no exciting hypotheses without fascinating constructs.

- Conceptualizing your research problem is critical to novel hypotheses. Here are a few simple guidelines:

  o Read good theoretical research: It is a rich source of research ideas.

  o Play with your ideas and concepts: Take risks, have fun, be inventive.

  o Develop your observation skills: Link your observations to theory.

  o Choose your concepts carefully: Anchor them in theory.

  o Push the limits of your concepts: Invent new ones when existing ones fail or fall short.

  o State your hypotheses clearly and concisely: Be wrong rather than unclear.

- Research should be fun—make it so!

CHECK YOUR UNDERSTANDING

In this chapter we generated about two dozen hypotheses as well as rationales for most of them. Now it is your turn. Below find a list of concepts:

Academic optimism

Cooperative learning

Dropout rate

Humanistic pupil control

Intelligence

Learning style

Open classroom climate

Organizational health

Professionalism

Student alienation

Student engagement

Teacher efficacy

Teacher engagement

Teacher mindfulness

Teacher morale

Teacher trust

Teaching method

Transformational leadership

1. From the above list, develop three testable hypotheses.

2. Diagram each of the hypotheses.

3. Develop an original hypothesis by selecting one concept from the list, and relate it to another construct not on the list, but one that you find intriguing. Make sure that your construct has a theoretical base.

4. Develop a sound theoretical argument (rationale) for your original hypothesis.

5. Can you develop a system of related hypotheses and present them in one theoretical model, such as the models found in Figures 5.1 or 5.2?

KEY TERMS

**Custodial
    orientation (p. 93)**

Dogmatism (p. 96)

**Humanistic
    orientation (p. 94)**

6

PRACTICAL APPLICATIONS

The final chapter of this book is a sample of some practical applications of quantitative analysis. To this point, our focus has been on the nature of science, its conceptual underpinnings, the foundations and understanding of statistical analyses, and the critique and generation of hypotheses. These elements of quantitative research are as essential for anyone expected to improve teaching and learning as they are for generating scientific knowledge. We illustrate the practical utility of quantitative analysis for practitioners. We do this by using the constructs of collective trust and organizational climate because in many organizations trust and climate are the keys to effective operation. Finally, we conclude with a set of specific guidelines for practitioners to improve and evaluate change.

COLLECTIVE TRUST

Knowledge about practice partly depends on access to accurate performance information. In Chapter 2 we mentioned the importance of using valid and reliable surveys to measure constructs. **Construct validity**, the ability of a measure to yield truthful judgments about the object it purports to capture, is the most important criteria for information quality (Messick, 1995; Miller, 2008). Even though there are different aspects of construct validity (content, predictive, discriminate, convergent, consequential, etc.), all share the same fundamental logic—that validity exists to the degree that the measure represents the underlining theoretical construct and informs credible judgments about the phenomenon of interest (Cronbach, 1971; Messick, 1995).

We use collective trust to illustrate considerations in selecting, using, and interpreting valid measures. We start with a conceptual definition. *Collective trust is a group's willingness to be vulnerable to another party based on the confidence that the party is benevolent, reliable, competent, honest, and open* (Forsyth, Adams, & Hoy, 2011; Tschannen-Moran & Hoy, 2000). Trust is embedded in relationships. The degree, for example, to which the faculty trusts its students, principal, parents, and each other yields a base for a picture of trust in schools. Review our discussion of trust in Chapter 2 for a more extended analysis of trust.

Culture of Trust

A prototype for a **culture of faculty trust** is one in which faculty trust is high on all referents of trust—principal, colleagues, students, and parents. First, teachers believe that the principal is trustworthy, consistently acts in their best interests, and is open, honest, reliable, and competent. The faculty also perceives their teacher colleagues as trustworthy if they are caring, competent, and authentic in their interactions with each other, and that even in difficult situations, they have learned to depend on each other with the confidence that their colleagues will not betray their trust. Faculty trust in students and parents is important in schools, perhaps critical. Surprisingly, research has consistently demonstrated that teachers do not distinguish between trusting students and parents (Bryk & Schneider, 2002; Forsyth, Adams, and Hoy; Hoy & Tschannen-Moran, 2003). When teachers trust students, they also trust parents and vice versa; consequently, the profile of trust that we describe in schools focuses on faculty trust in the principal, colleagues, and clients (students and parents). Faculty trust in students and parents is strong if the teachers believe students are capable of learning and that parents and students are truthful, reliable, dependable, open, and caring.

These three referents of trust (principal, colleagues, and students and parents) are often moderately correlated with each other; that is, trust or distrust tends to permeate the school. Yet, it is quite possible for the faculty to trust each other and the principal and not to trust the students and parents or to trust colleagues, but not the principal. In brief, a strong culture of organizational trust in schools is one in which the faculty trusts the principal, faculty members trust each other, and the faculty trusts both students and parents; consequently, all groups work together in a spirit of harmony and cooperation (Hoy & Miskel, 2013).

Measuring Organizational Trust

It is relatively easy to get a quick snapshot of faculty trust using the **Omnibus T-Scale**, developed by Hoy and Tschannen-Moran (2003). Remember that trust is the faculty's willingness to be vulnerable to another party based on the confidence that the latter party is benevolent, reliable, competent, honest, and open; in other words that the party is trustworthy. Effective for all school levels—elementary, middle, and high school—the 26-item Omnibus T-Scale measures the three referents of faculty trust that we just described as trust in principal, trust in colleagues, and trust in clients (parents and students). Examples of items on the trust scale include the following:

- The principal typically acts in the best interests of teachers. (Trust in principal)

- The principal in this school is competent doing his or her job. (Trust in principal)

- Students in this school can be counted on to do their work. (Trust in clients)

- Parents in this school are reliable in their commitments. (Trust in clients)

- Teachers in this school typically look out for each other. (Trust in colleagues)

The Omnibus T-Scale is a valid and reliable 26-item scale (Hoy & Tschannen-Moran, 2003) that can be found at www.waynekhoy.com. Simply download the scale, make copies, and it is ready to use. Teachers are asked to describe along a 6-point Likert scale the extent to which they agree with the statements from strongly disagree to agree. It is best to administer the scale in a faculty meeting and ensure complete anonymity. The scoring directions are found on the website and are easy to follow. In brief, the items are grouped into three sets, one for each of the aspects of school trust. They are averaged and summed to get a collective score for faculty trust in the principal, faculty trust in colleagues, and faculty trust in clients (students and parents).

I suggest you revisit the section in Chapter 2 on standard scores and normal distributions because to make the scores easily interpretable, the trust scores on the Omnibus T-scale are reported as standard scores rather than raw scores. A quick review of standard scores may be helpful. Recall that **standard scores** are based on the standard deviation of a distribution.

A **z score** is a specific type of standard score that indicates how many standard deviations above or below the mean a score falls. A z score of 0 means the score is equal to the mean whereas a z score of 1 represents a score exactly 1 standard deviation above the mean and z score of -1 is a score exactly 1 standard deviation below the mean. *To transform any raw score to a z score, use the formula $z = x/s$ where x is the (raw score minus the mean) or as we have learned the deviation from the mean, and s is the standard deviation of the sample.* For example, if your score is 125 in a set of test scores with a mean of 100 and a standard deviation of 25, then your z score would be one, [(raw score-mean) divided by the standard deviation, that is (125-100)/25 = 1]. Your test score is 1 standard deviation above the mean; your score is higher than 84%

of those who took the test. Review Figure 3.1 in Chapter 3. There are many kinds of standard scores in addition to z scores. For example, IQ scores are reported as standard scores with a mean of 100 and a standard deviation of 15. If your IQ is 145, then you are a genius! Your IQ is 3 standard deviations above the mean—greater than 99% of the people.

To make it easy to interpret scores on the Omnibus T-Scale, the scoring directions have you standardize the raw scores based on typical normative data of schools collected earlier. These standard scores have a mean of 500 and a standard deviation of 100. For example, if your school score is 700 on faculty trust in the principal, the score is two standard deviations above the average score on faculty trust in the principal for of all schools in the sample; that is, the school has more faculty trust in colleagues than 97% of the schools in the sample. You may recognize this system as the one used in reporting individual scores on the Scholastic Aptitude Tests (SATs), College Entrance Examination Board (CEEBs), and the Graduate Record Examinations (GREs). The range of these scores is presented below:

- If the score is 200, it is lower than 99% of the schools

- If the score is 300, it is lower than 97% of the schools

- If the score is 400, it is lower than 84% of the schools

- If the score is 500, it is average

- If the score is 600, it is higher than 84% of the schools

- If the score is 700, it is higher than 97% of the schools

- If the score is 800, it is higher than 99% of the schools

If you follow the standardized scoring procedures on our web page (www.waynekhoy .com), you can tell at a glance where your school falls along the normal probability curve. In other words, you have a base on which to compare the trust in your schools with typical schools in the normative sample. The higher the score, the greater the faculty trust in your school, and any score greater than 500 is above average in trust compared to the other schools in the sample. Standard scores give you a common standard, which makes it easy to compare your scores with each other as well as with other schools.

You could proceed the same way for measuring student and parent trust. Forsyth, Adams, and Hoy (2011) have developed valid and reliable scales to measure these forms of trust, which are also available and described at www.waynekhoy.com. Example items include the following:

- The principal at my school likes students. (Student item for trust in principal)

- Teachers in this school really listen to students. (Student item for trust in teachers)

- At this school I know I will be listened to. (Parent item for trust in school)

- The principal is always honest. (Parent item for trust in principal)

Administer these anonymous questionnaires to representative sets of parents and students, score them, and develop an enhanced school profile. The scoring directions, including standardization procedures, are also found on line at www.waynekhoy .com. A school profile of trust can be developed using the results of these sets of trust instruments. For example, we replicated a **trust profile** for an actual elementary school and use that profile below to illustrate how to describe and interpret trust found in that organization.

Trust Profile for an Elementary School	
• Faculty Trust in Teachers	562
• Faculty Trust in Principal	502
• Faculty Trust in Students and Parents	499
Average Faculty Trust	**521**
• Student Trust in Teachers	489
• Student Trust in Principal	499
Average Student Trust	**494**
• Parent Trust in School	489
• Parent Trust in Principal	497
Average Parent Trust	**493**

Interpreting Organizational Trust Profiles

How do we interpret the numbers in this organizational trust profile? What do the numbers mean? Most of the scores above are near the mean of the normative sample (500)—the sample on which the scoring comparisons are derived. First, let's examine the trust of the faculty. An overall average of 521 indicates that faculty trust in this school is just slightly better than average. Closer scrutiny of the school's profile, however, shows that teachers tend to trust each other much more than they do the principal or students and parents. Further, the faculty trust in each other (i.e., their colleagues) is the factor that is pulling the overall trust above average. How would you feel about the trust profile if this were your school? As principal you might start with a plan to improve faculty trust in parents and students. After all, it is faculty trust in clients that makes the difference with respect to student achievement (Forsyth, Adams, & Hoy, 2011). Perhaps by figuring out why teachers don't trust the principal as much as they do their colleagues, you may gain some insight into changing the culture of trust in this school. Do you think it is possible to increase faculty trust in parents and students without improving their trust in the principal?

At this point, it might be enlightening for you as principal to respond to the Omnibus T-Scale yourself and then score it the same way you did the teacher scales. Scoring is easy because you need not average any scores for yourself. Now compare your judgment with the scores of your teachers. Our experience is that principals see themselves as a lot more trustworthy than their teachers see them. Why do you think that is? Can you test your speculation? How?

A few things should be clear to you now. First, overall trust is at best a rough gauge of faculty trust. Second, the breakdown of faculty trust into the three referent groups provides a more refined and useful picture. The entire profile should help you map a more precise strategy of action. Finally, the numbers give a quick picture of the school's culture of trust, but action based on these numbers requires reflection. Numbers are not enough. What they mean and what is happening to produce the patterns are critical. Answers to these questions often require more information and careful consideration.

One would expect that faculty trust in students and parents would in turn lead to parental and student trust in the school and the principal. So, next we turn to student trust—the degree to which students trust the teachers and the principal. Here the profile of trust in our elementary school reveals that again our school is average in trust; the overall average student trust score is 494. But again, if we examine the two scores individually, we see that although the students have an average trust in the principal, their appraisal of the trustworthiness of teachers is slightly below average. We wonder why?

Finally, we turn to parent trust—the degree to which parents trust the school and the principal. The overall parental trust score is about average (493); however, although parents have average trust in the principal (497), parental trust in the school is slightly below average (489).

In sum, the trust levels in this elementary school are near average, but in some key aspects of trust, the profile suggests there is work to be done building trust because the scores suggest slightly below average levels of trust, especially in the areas of student trust in teachers and in parental trust in the school. Moreover, how satisfied are you with average trust scores? The scales and numbers sketch a quick picture of trust, and the process raises a host of questions that perceptive and mindful teachers and administrators would find intriguing and worthy of investigation. For those interested in strategies for improving a culture of trust in schools, we suggest reading Forsyth, Adams, and Hoy (2011).

ORGANIZATIONAL CLIMATE

As we examine the climate of schools, let's look at one more example of quantitative analysis that illustrates the utility of standard scores, constitutive and operational definitions, percentiles, and the normal curve. In Chapter 2 we discussed the concept of school climate. **School climate** is the "personality of the school," defined by the leadership of the principal, and the interactions of the teachers.

Climate of Openness

An open school climate is defined by open, authentic interactions among teachers and between the principal and teachers. The openness of the principal's behavior is examined in terms of the following three kinds of interaction patterns.

- *Supportive* principal behavior is action that reflects basic concern for teachers, help and respect for teachers, and general openness in interactions with teachers.

- *Directive* principal behavior is rigid, close, controlling supervision of teachers.

- *Restrictive* principal behavior hinders rather than facilitates teacher work; the principal burdens teachers with reports, meetings, and busywork.

In brief, openness of the leadership is behavior that is supportive, nondirective, and not restrictive. Accordingly, the leader's behavior is respectful, helpful, and genuine as well as positive, encouraging, and free of unnecessary demands and restrictions.

Next, consider the interaction patterns of the teachers in terms of how they relate with each other. As with the principal-teacher interactions, the following are three major patterns of teacher-teacher interactions.

- *Collegial* behavior is teacher behavior that is open, professional, accepting, and respectful: Teachers are proud of their school and respect the professional competence of their colleagues.

- *Intimate* behavior reflects a cohesive and strong network of social support: Teachers know each other well, socialize with each other, and are good friends.

- *Disengaged* behavior refers to a lack of meaning and focus in teacher professional work: Teachers are simply going through the motions and are not committed to teaching.

Openness of the teacher-teacher interactions is characterized by professional and respectful exchanges among teachers as well as a cohesive and strong network of social support and commitment to engaging in the work of the group. Note that the six previous concepts describe the school in terms of principal and teacher behavior; the underlying conception is open and authentic interaction patterns.

An *open school climate* is one in which the principal's leadership is supportive, nondirective, and not restrictive. Teachers respond with a commitment to teaching and learning, close intimate social relations, and collegial relations among themselves. There is a genuine and authentic character to the open and transparent relationships in the professional activities of the school. This latter construct, school openness, is the most general and inclusive of the six earlier concepts.

To summarize, schools give different initial impressions to observers; we sense the feel or tone of the school even in brief visits. How do we "get a handle" on this feeling of schools? We call this ambience the organizational climate of the schools. We likened the school climate to the personality of an individual; that is, *climate is to organization what personality is to individual.* In our framework for school climate, we defined the basic indicators of school climate: supportive, nondirective, nonrestrictive principal behavior and collegial, intimate, and engaged teacher behavior. Finally, we defined an open school climate in terms of these six school characteristics. Clearly, this is not the only perspective to view school climate; in fact, others may be more useful to you depending on what you want to study. Good reviews of other perspectives on school climate and culture are found in the work of Hoy and his colleagues (Hoy & Miskel, 2008; Hoy & Sabo, 1998; Hoy, Tarter, & Kottkamp, 1991).

Measuring Organizational Climate

Because we have reviewed the conceptual meaning of school climate, we can now turn to the operational measures of school climate, which in this case emphasizes the openness of the teacher interactions as well as the teacher-principal relations. We can operationalize these concepts by using reliable and valid measures of each of the concepts. The openness of school climate is measured by the **Organizational Climate Description Questionnaire (OCDQ)**, which is gauged by a serious of Likert-type questions along a 4-point scale from "rarely occurs" to "frequently occurs." There are three versions of this scale—one for elementary, middle, and high schools. The OCDQ is available on line at www.waynekhoy.com along with the directions for administering and scoring the various elements of climate.

Below we give you a representative sample of an item on each scale. Respondents are asked to describe the behavior of the principal or teacher on a scale from "rarely" to "frequently occurs."

- *Supportive behavior*: The principal listens to and supports teachers' suggestions.

- *Directive behavior*: The principal rules with an iron fist.

- *Restrictive behavior*: Teachers are burdened with busy work.

Likewise teachers are asked to describe their interactions with each other.

- *Collegial behavior*: Teachers help and support each other.

- *Intimate behavior*: Teachers socialize with each other on a regular basis.

- *Disengaged behavior*: Faculty meetings are useless.

In addition to school scores on the six climate dimensions, three more general openness scores can be computed: openness of the principal's behavior, openness of teacher-principal behavior, and overall school openness. A note in scoring the OCDQ for elementary schools: To compute the openness measures—directive, restrictive, and disengaged are reversed scored. This reversal of the score converts directive into nondirective; restrictive into nonrestrictive; and disengaged into engaged. Simply follow the directions on the web page and the subtests will be reversed to get the openness indices. Thus, principal openness refers to supportive, nondirective, and nonrestrictive behavior, and open teacher behavior is collegial, intimate, and engaged behavior.

Interpreting Organizational Climate Profiles

You should be able to describe the organizational climate of a school. Can you? Examine the organization profile of the elementary school below. Remember that all the scores are reported as standard scores with a mean of 500 and a standard deviation of 100 for easy comparisons. These scores are normed so that 500 represents an average score and a score of 600 represents a school score one standard deviation about the average score whereas a score of 300 represents indicates a school two standard deviations below the average school score.

Let's turn to the organizational climate profile below of an actual elementary school with 26 teachers. What jumps out as you examine this profile of organizational climate scores? First, the principal is quite supportive of teachers in the school (558) and clearly above average. Continuing to examine the principal's behavior, we see that this principal is below average in being directive (422); he or she encourages teachers to use their initiative. The principal does not supervise teachers closely, but rather gives them autonomy to make professional decisions. Finally, the principal does not burden teachers with busy work or unnecessary meetings; the principal is below average in restrictive behavior (440). All in all, the principal's score on openness of 565 (calculated by following the directions for reversing the directive and restrictive subtests) is significantly better than most: in fact, the score is more that a half a standard deviation above the average for most principals.

Organizational Openness Profile for an Elementary School	
• Supportive principal behavior	558
• Directive principal behavior	422
• Restrictive principal behavior	440
Openness of principal behavior	565
• Collegial teacher behavior	498
• Intimate teacher behavior	504
• Disengaged teacher behavior	510
Openness of teacher behavior	497
Overall Index of Openness	531

Next let's interpret the openness of the teachers' behavior. The overall openness of teacher interactions is average (498). In fact, all the openness scores for the teachers are about average. Collegial behavior is average (498), intimate behavior is average (497), and disengaged behavior is slightly higher than average (510). Unfortunately, disengaged behavior is the opposite of openness, but fortunately, the score is still near average.

If we average the two openness scores for the school, we see that the school is slightly above average in openness (531). The openness of score, however, is skewed to the positive side by the actions of the principal. In other words, the teachers' behaviors (497) are not nearly as open as the principal's (565). If you were the leader of this organization, you would realize that you need to work on reducing the disengagement of teachers (510) and then develop some strategies to improve collegial behavior (498) as teachers engage in the task at hand. Also you might encourage activities that lead to more social cohesiveness and intimacy (504) among the group. The principal is "out in front" of the teachers in openness. The question is what the leader can do to move the teachers toward more openness, that is, more collegial and intimate behavior and less disengagement in their work.

GUIDELINES FOR IMPROVEMENT

Finally, we advance a set of guidelines that help professionals build knowledge about improvement by using the tools of quantitative research to study problems of practice. To this point in the chapter, using examples of collective trust and organizational climate, we demonstrate that the use of quantitative research is not limited to social scientists. Professionals can use the elements of quantitative research to study and improve practice. In fact, the generation of practical knowledge has now become the central focus of improvement science. We conclude with a brief description of improvement science and a set of guidelines for advancing practice in a systematic way.

Improvement Science

Improvement science organizes planned change by a process similar to that of building generalizable knowledge about natural phenomena. The emphasis on science recognizes the critical role that knowledge generation plays in understanding how social systems like schools operate more effectively (Langley et al., 2010). Improvement science sets as the object of study the practices and processes used to make teaching and learning measurably better. A move toward science as a process to lead and manage improvement fundamentally shifts how educators and other professionals think about and implement change. Rather than looking to the external environment for what works, improvement science builds capacity within schools and organizations to learn continuously from practice (Bryk, 2009).

Educators cannot generate practical knowledge about their actions without using the elements of quantitative research that we described in previous chapters. Whether improvement is for the entry year teacher struggling to engage students in critical thinking or the large school district aiming to build professional capacity, the scientific process applied to educational practice harnesses knowledge creation and learning as the engine of reform. Bryk (2009) argues, "you can't improve practice at scale unless you measure it and unless the evidence base is organized around some working theory about how various instructional processes, organizing routines, and cultural norms interact to affect desired outcomes" (p. 598).

Improvement science is organized around action research, and for a long time action research has promoted inquiry on problems of practice as a means to understand the complex social and human processes at the center of effective schooling. Lewin (1946) first introduced *action research* as a collaborative process between researchers and practitioners. The purpose was to build theory about change in social systems by studying the effects of human behavior in their natural contexts (Lewin, 1946; Rapoport, 1970). Action research is as useful for practitioners as it is for researchers. Educators looking to improve teaching and learning need to understand the effects of their practices on performance (Checkland & Holwell, 1998).

Improvement Science Cycle: Plan-Do-Study-Act (PDSA)

Improvement science applies the principles of action research through **Plan-Do-Study-Act** (PDSA) **Cycles**. Langley and his associates (2010) describe the cycle in detail. Edwards Deming (2000) used PDSA cycles to transform Japanese car manufacturing from a struggling industry in the 1960's into the current gold standard of organizational performance. The success of Deming's approach spawned a quality movement that continues to revolutionize manufacturing and is now transforming healthcare. Led by the Institute for Healthcare Improvement (IHI), the regular use of PDSA cycles is credited for dramatically reducing error in hospitals and greatly enhancing the delivery of patient care (Kenny, 2008).

At its core, PDSA follows the scientific approach we described in Chapter 1. Knowledge creation starts with theory, theory informs hypotheses, hypotheses are tested systematically, new evidence is used to revise or elaborate theory, and new hypotheses are advanced then tested again. PDSA builds practical knowledge through a similar cyclical process (Figure 6.1):

- *Planning* is developing a set of assumptions (theory) that explains how change will lead to improvement;

- *Doing* involves making observations and measuring change as plans are implemented;

- *Studying* means evaluating the evidence to determine if change has resulted in improvement; and

- *Acting* entails going public with the evidence and revising the original plans if needed.

Figure 6.1   Comparison of the Scientific Process and PDSA Cycle

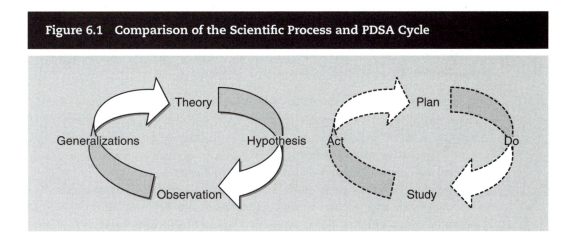

Both individuals and organizations improve performance by learning from their actions, but learning from practice is more easily espoused than lived. Established routines, external pressure, and other factors often impede efforts to study systematically processes, practices, and outcomes. For this reason, we offer five guidelines for professionals in schools and other organizations about how to use improvement science to study and lead change. These guidelines derive from the tools of quantitative research described in previous chapters.

Guideline 1: View problems as questions about performance issues

In Chapter 2 we noted that a research problem is a query about the relationship between two or more variables. Problems in schools and other organizations are seldom thought of as questions; they are viewed as deficiencies that need fixing. Practitioners fall into the trap of searching for interventions that work before they sort out plausible reasons for the problem in the first place. Even though there may be an urgency to fix an ineffective system, we advise studying the issue prior to arriving at a simple solution. The first step is an accurate diagnosis of the situation. Problems stated as questions encourage a deeper examination of the contexts, issues, and opportunities facing organizations. Just as research problems spark curiosity, problems of practice should provoke a desire to understand what lies beneath the observable signs of an issue.

In their work on the scholarship of teaching and learning, Huber and Hutchings (2005) argued that serious improvement begins at the same starting place as good research with a question that moves individuals toward a meaningful understanding of what, how, and why something is happening. Questions about performance issues lead individuals in search of theory and evidence related to the specific concern. For example, if achievement disparities exist in a school, we want to know why they may exist before a strategy is devised or an intervention adopted. The answer to questions about cause, reason, or purpose (why questions) depends in part on a general theoretical explanation for the existence of achievement gaps.

So, what types of questions should you ask? What, why, and how questions are ideal. These questions provoke conversations that elaborate different assumptions and perspectives about processes, practices, and outcomes that need improving. Such questions also steer conversations toward investigation of the human and social mechanisms essential for improvement to occur. To illustrate, an improvement tool like performance-based teacher evaluation does not work on its own to enhance classroom instruction; its effectiveness is a function of how it is used. Evidence on adult learning theory, motivation, and expertise development builds knowledge about those actions that can maximize the use of evaluations. Our point is that general, conceptual knowledge informs a line of reasoning for the effective use of improvement strategies or interventions. Problems framed as questions encourage individuals and groups to understand the issue before constructing a course of action.

Guideline 2: Think of improvement strategies as theories that require testing

Organizations learn by creating knowledge and knowledge requires theory. We agree with Edwards Deming (2000) that "Without theory there is no way to use the information that comes to us on the instant" (p. 106). A theory for how change is predicted to unfold establishes a conceptual framework to study practice. Improvement strategies or interventions are not theories, but they can be part of a logical explanation for how and why change is predicted to make performance better.

A mistake we see played out in many settings is to think of improvement as a simple process of adopting an intervention. Improvement is anything but simple. Good ideas and new initiatives will fail to accomplish their goals if relevant evidence is not continuously informing the decision-making process. Theory building brings to the surface different ideas, knowledge, and beliefs about improvement and how change is expected to unfold. You cannot improve something unless you can measure it, and you can't measure change unless you have a framework that specifies the pathway to better outcomes.

Figure 6.2 is illustrative of a theory for how deeper learning in math occurs. It is assumed that student trust in teachers and student engagement are preconditions for deeper learning. Just as you are more likely to invest your money when you trust your financial advisor, students are more likely to invest their cognitive and motivational resources when they trust their teacher. Standards-based assessments and problem-based instruction are likely to enhance student trust and engagement, which in turn lead to deeper learning.

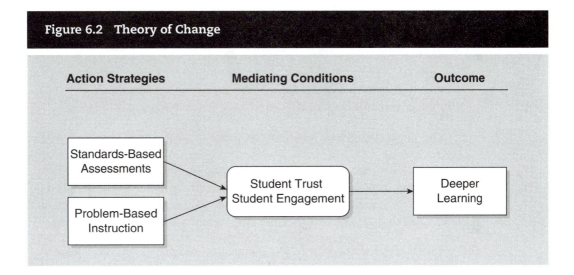

Figure 6.2   Theory of Change

To construct such a theory, we begin with an outcome (Langley et. al., 2010). The following questions are helpful:

- What are we trying to accomplish?

- How will we know if improvement occurs?

Deep learning in math can be defined, it is specific, and it represents a growing expectation that schools prepare students to think critically, conceptualize problems, work collaboratively, and apply knowledge and skills to solve complex problems.

With an outcome set, our thinking shifts to conditions that are directly related to the objective. For deeper math learning, students need to be engaged and trust their teachers. The following questions are helpful:

- What conditions lead to the outcome (i.e., in our example, deeper learning)?

- What evidence supports the relationship between the conditions and the outcome?

Student engagement and trust are two mediating conditions that lead to deeper learning. How do we know this? General evidence links both student engagement and trust to motivation, learning, and achievement (Adams, 2014; Klem & Connell, 2004; Marks, 2000).

Action strategies complete the theory of change because they set a clear direction for performance (Connell & Klem, 2000; Honig & Hatch, 2004). Questions to identify action strategies include:

- What changes can lead to mediating conditions, such as student engagement and trust?

- Does evidence support the effectiveness of the proposed changes?

The explanation of improvement (Figure 6.2) should be questioned for its plausibility and testability (Connell & Klem, 2000). Is the logic underlying the model sound? If not, you need to rethink the explanation. The model cannot be tested without valid and reliable measures. In other words, can the concepts be defined and operationalized?

Rather than merely looking for solutions, or interventions that "work," begin with the construction of a theory of change that lays out the explanatory evidence on how something works. Over 50 years of education research tells us that understanding *why and how* plans work has more utility for practitioners than simply knowing *if* something works (Bryk, 2009; Forsyth, Adams, & Hoy, 2011; Spillane, Gomez, & Mesler, 2009).

Guideline 3: Measure mediating conditions and outcomes

Performance decisions are susceptible to error with outcome only measures. Knowledge about improvement requires valid and reliable measures of mediating conditions as well as final outcomes. Results tell very little about performance in cases where tasks are complex. We need accurate information to understand if the proposed action strategies are leading to better performance.

Valid performance judgments depend on a body of comprehensive data accumulated over time, not simply data collected at the beginning and end of the intervention. Herein lies a problem. Time is a scarce resource. Educators need immediate feedback about action strategies, and measures of mediating conditions are useful in this regard because they provide intermediate evidence to assess the progress of action plans. Positive changes in mediating conditions signal the likely effectiveness of new practices.

Recall from Chapter 2 that once concepts are given definitions they can be transformed into variables. Deeper learning is defined as thinking critically, solving complex problems, working collaboratively, communicating effectively, and directing one's own learning (Alliance for Excellent Education, 2011; Chow, 2010). Clearly deep learning is complex; it consists of different elements, each of which can be turned into variables through a set of operations. Likewise, student engagement and trust can also be defined and measured (Appleton, Christenson, & Furlong, 2008; Archambault, Janosz, Fallu, & Pagani, 2009; Forsyth, Adams, & Hoy, 2011; Marks, 2000).

A caveat is in order. Remember Campbell's Law: "The more any quantitative social indicator is used for social decision-making, the more subject it will be to corruption and pressures and the more apt it will be to distort and corrupt the social processes it is intended to monitor" (Campbell, 1976, p. 35). Thus as you measure mediating conditions and outcomes, guard against possible distortions and corruptions of decision making by also using non-quantitative information to guide the process.

Guideline 4: Turn information into knowledge by analyzing the data

We now see how theories of change and performance measures guide the collection of improvement data. However, data and information should not be confused with knowledge. These are distinct constructs that exist at very different levels and degrees within organizations. For instance, data are raw numbers or symbols that lack meaning in and of themselves. Information is contextual; that is, to have meaning data need a point of reference or context. For example, 50 is a raw number, a data point, which has meaning only in terms of its reference or context. A 50 out of 50 is typically outstanding, whereas a 50% is not so good. Simply collecting information does not produce knowledge.

Data need to be analyzed, and the appropriate analytical technique depends on the questions that are asked. Questions about implementation of action strategies and their effectiveness are well suited for quantitative techniques. For implementation, practitioners need to know if mediating conditions are moving in the predicted direction. For example, the following question might be stated: Is student engagement improving with the use of problem-based learning? Little to no change in engagement either suggests an implementation problem or the selection of an inappropriate action strategy. The only way to know is to analyze the data.

We described several analytical techniques in Chapter 3 that are helpful for examining patterns in the data. Measures of central tendencies can describe changes in average student engagement over time. A standard score of student engagement (e.g., a z score) can be used to compare the relative rank of student engagement in this school with others. For example, earlier in this chapter, we used a standard score of 500 to indicate an average school score.

Effectiveness questions are meant to determine if results are consistent with expectations, that is, with the proposed explanation (theory). We need to know how to determine if intended outcomes are realized and if they can be attributed to the change. An effectiveness question might be stated as follows: Do mathematical knowledge and skills improve over time? Descriptive data can be used to describe mean differences over time, and then t-tests and ANOVA can be used to test the likelihood that differences are the result of chance.

Attribution seeks to determine the extent to which the action strategies contributed to the results (McDavid & Hawthorn, 2006). Certainty about the actual causes of outcomes is not possible, yet we must address attribution questions. For improvement science, we want to know if the weight of the evidence suggests that outcomes can be attributed to the planned change. Evidence on the implementation of action strategies and measures of mediating conditions are useful in building a case for attribution. For example, if math achievement increases, but student engagement drops, then it is incumbent on us to figure out what is happening. Clearly, the dynamics of change are not occurring as expected.

Guideline 5: Go public with the evidence

Knowledge of planned change is only useful if it leads to purposeful action. Now that data have been analyzed and evidence reported, it is only natural to want to act quickly on the findings. Evidence supporting the theory of change would seem to justify swift plans to scale-up the initiative whereas disconfirming evidence would suggest quick revisions to action strategies. Hasty decisions should not be the first reaction to the findings. Instead, the first response should be to go public with the evidence by submitting it to a community of peers and stakeholders for review (Hatch, 2006). This action need not be as formal nor take as long as the peer review process for scientific research, but the principle of vetting evidence by peers and stakeholders is a good way to test the accuracy and acceptance of conclusions.

The public review will look different depending on the context and nature of change. A teacher experimenting with problem-based instruction may share evidence with her teaching colleagues in the school. A school undergoing comprehensive reform may share evidence with the larger community and other schools connected in a reform network. There are many outlets for practice-based evidence that should be used to test the findings and conclusions before making decisions to either refine the explanation or to scale-up the initiative.

To conclude, Table 6.1 shows the relationship between the five guidelines and the PDSA cycle of improvement. Guidelines 1 and 2 set targets for the planning. Guideline 3 calls attention to mediating conditions and outcomes in the selection of performance measures. Guideline 4 emphasizes the importance of turning information into knowledge. Guideline 5 identifies the importance of acting on the evidence by being transparent and going public with the findings.

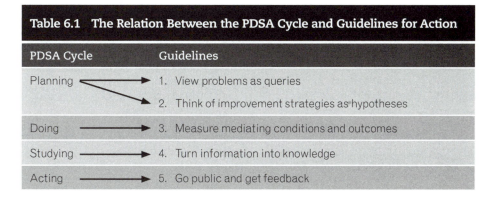

Table 6.1   The Relation Between the PDSA Cycle and Guidelines for Action

PDSA Cycle	Guidelines
Planning	1. View problems as queries
	2. Think of improvement strategies as hypotheses
Doing	3. Measure mediating conditions and outcomes
Studying	4. Turn information into knowledge
Acting	5. Go public and get feedback

SUMMARY

This chapter provides examples of some practical applications of quantitative research. The following propositions are key:

- Construct validity is the ability of a measure to yield truthful judgments about the object it purports to capture.

- An organizational culture of trust is one in which trust is pervasive among its role members. For example, in schools, faculty trust is strong on all its referents—principal, colleagues, and students and parents.

- The Omnibus T-scale is a valid and reliable measure of the trustworthiness of principals, colleagues, and students and parents.

- A z score is a specific type of standard score that indicates how many standard deviations above or below the mean a score falls.

- For our measures of collective trust and school climate, we use standard scores with a mean of 500 and a standard deviation of 100 to create school profiles.

- School climate is the "personality of the school," defined by the leadership of the principal and the interactions of the teachers.

- The organizational climate of schools can be described in a number of ways. We use openness of both principal-teacher relations and teacher-teacher interactions to define the openness of school climates.

- The Organizational Climate Description Questionnaire (OCDQ) is a reliable and valid measure of the openness of school climate.

- Improvement science is a systematic form of action research that stresses a cycle of planning, doing, studying, and acting (PDSA).

The chapter concludes with five guidelines for teachers and administrators as they use improvement science for positive change in schools:

1. View problems as questions of performance.

2. View improvement strategies as hypotheses for testing.

3. Measure mediating conditions and outcomes.

4. Transform information into knowledge.

5. Go public and get feedback before acting on the evidence.

CHECK YOUR UNDERSTANDING

1. What is validity? Go back to Chapter 2 to check the definition of reliable. What is the difference between a measure's reliability and validity?

2. What is a z score? What is a standard score? How do you interpret a standard score of 650 if the mean is 500 and standard deviation is 100? How would you interpret a standard score of 115 if the mean is 100 and the standard deviation is 15? What percentage of the scores in a normal distribution is greater than one standard deviation above the mean?

3. What is the difference between a constitutive and operational definition? What is our constitutive definition of collective trust? What is the operational definition of collective trust? Give examples of constitutive and operational definitions for organizational climate.

4. What is improvement science? What is the PDSA Cycle?

5. There are a number of ways to measure the organizational climate. One is to use the **Organizational Health Inventory (OHI)**. If you measured the organizational health of a

high school using the OHI-S (i.e., S represents for a secondary school; see www.waynekhoy.com) and found the organizational health profile that is indicated below, write a brief descriptive narrative of the health of the school. What aspects of the health profile need improvement and why? Suggest a few things a leader might do to improve the health of the school.

The Organizational Health Profile of a Secondary School	
• Institutional Integrity	450
• Initiating Structure	450
• Consideration	650
• Principal Influence	530
• Resource Support	510
• Morale	525
• Academic Emphasis	450
Overall Health Index	**509**

Institutional Integrity is the degree to which the educational program is unimpeded by disruptive external forces.

Initiating Structure is the degree to which the leader structures task-oriented behavior.

Consideration is the degree to which the leader looks out for the welfare of organizational participants.

Principal Influence is the degree to which the leader has "pull" with superiors.

Resource Support is the degree to which the organization has the necessary resources needed to succeed.

Morale is the degree to which teachers feel good about each other and at the same time feel a sense of accomplishment.

Academic Emphasis is the degree of press for academic and intellectual accomplishment.

KEY TERMS

Collective trust (p. 113)
Construct validity (p. 113)
Culture of faculty trust (p. 114)
Improvement science (p. 123)
Omnibus T-Scale (p. 114)
Openness of
   school climate (p. 121)

Organizational
   Climate Descriptive
   Questionnaire
   (OCDQ) (p. 121)
Organizational
   Health Index (OHI) (p. 132)
PDSA cycle (p. 124)

School climate (p. 119)
Standard score (p. 115)
Trust profile (p. 117)
Z score (p. 115)

APPENDIX A

Elements of a Proposal

This appendix has a basic purpose: *To give beginning students direction for developing a quantitative research proposal.* A proposal has three major sections:

1. The introduction

2. The review of the literature and generation of hypotheses

3. The design and method of the study

The proposal document varies from a concise statement to a more comprehensive description of the research project. In some graduate schools, the latter takes the form of the first three chapters of a dissertation, illustrated below.

PART 1: THE INTRODUCTION (CHAPTER 1)

- *Overview:* Start with a general overview of the chapter. In a paragraph, describe the organization of the chapter.

- *Background of the study:* This is a brief section, usually only a page or two, that frames the study in terms of contemporary developments in the field. Provide the general setting of the study, and foreshadow your research problem.

- *Need and purpose:* This is an extension of the background; however, it is more specific. Why is this particular study needed? What is the purpose of the study? Create interest, and convince the reader that this is an important area. What is the theoretical, research, and practical significance of the study?

- *Definition of concepts:* Briefly define each of the important terms and concepts of the study. The definition of terms should be linked to the specific way that you use the terms and should be consistent with usage in the extant research and theory.

- *Statement of the research problem:* What are the general questions and/or hypotheses that guide your study? Make certain you clearly state the questions that you are trying to answer. In the literature review, usually the second chapter of your dissertation, develop a logical argument for your proposed hypotheses to answer the research questions.

- *Scope and limitations:* What is the scope of your study? In other words, how narrow or broad are you going to make your study? For example, the study may focus on only elementary teachers in Ohio who responded to your research instruments.

> What are the limitations? *Limitations* refer to potential weaknesses of the study. For example, what are the shortcomings of the sample or the measures? Is self-selection of respondents a problem? Are those who responded to the study different from those who did not respond? It is best for you to describe the weaknesses of the research yourself.

- *Summary:* Summarize the elements of this chapter in a paragraph or two.

PART 2: THE LITERATURE REVIEW (CHAPTER 2)

- *Overview:* Start with a general overview of the chapter. In a paragraph, describe the organization of the chapter.

- *Conceptual framework:* Review the literature for each concept.

> Define each concept.

> Review its historical and conceptual underpinnings.

> Examine the empirical and theoretical research.

> Draw conclusions from the review for each concept.

- *Theory:* The conceptual framework should culminate with a synthesis of the undergirding theory driving the study.

- *Hypotheses or questions of the study:* Develop a theoretical rationale for each of the research hypotheses. Make sure that each hypothesis is concise, clear, and testable.

> The *rationale* is the system of logic and evidence that leads you to a specific question or supports the proposed hypothesis. Each hypothesis should have a theoretical rationale, that is, a logical argument of the theory and research that supports the hypothesis.

> A *research question* asks what the relationship is between two or more variables—it is an interrogative. Research questions often guide

exploratory studies, but it is best if you can determine the likely answers to the questions based on the extant research and theory, that is, develop a set of hypotheses.

A *hypothesis* answers a research question; it is a declarative statement that indicates the relation between two or more variables. State the hypothesis in substantive form, not the null form.

A *model* is a theoretical explanation of the relations that often encompass a number of hypotheses. Sometimes, a carefully crafted theoretical argument can produce a framework that synthesizes the assumptions and hypotheses into one coherent explanation, which is called a model. Not all studies will test a model because there may simply not be enough known or suspected information or research to create a model.

- *Summary:* Summarize the chapter in a paragraph or two.

PART 3: METHODOLOGY (CHAPTER 3)

- *Overview:* Start with a brief overview of the chapter.

- *Sample:* Describe the sample, how it was selected, and the rationale for its selection. How representative is your sample of the population (the target group you use to generalize your findings)?

- *Design:* If your study is an experimental study, then provide the details of the experimental design of the study.

What are the experimental and control groups of the study?

How are these groups determined?

Is there random assignment to groups and selection of groups?

What is the experimental treatment? Describe it.

How will the researcher manipulate the independent variable?

How will the dependent variables be measured?

- *Data collection:* Describe the data collection procedures; that is, how will the data be collected?

- *Measures:* For each variable, describe its measure.

  What kind of measure (e.g., a Likert scale) is it?

  Provide a sample of items and the response set for the items.

  Provide evidence of reliability and validity for each measure.

  Describe any pilot studies that were done to develop or refine the measures.

  Provide the full measure in the appendix.

- *Statistics:* Describe the statistical analyses that will be used to answer each research question or to test each hypothesis. Provide a rationale for the use of each statistic.

- *Summary:* Summarize what was done in this chapter in a paragraph.

APPENDIX B

A Few Writing Tips

- Keep your writing *simple and concise*; don't try to impress the reader with your vocabulary.

- Be *clear*. When the argument is complex or abstract, provide *concrete examples* to illustrate. *Clarity* is a key to good writing.

- Prefer the *active voice*; it is more direct and forceful.
  - Poor—The research method was explained by Tarter (1998).
  - *Better*—Tarter (1998) explained the research method.

- Use the *past tense* to express something that has occurred in the past, as when discussing another researcher's work and when reporting your results.
  - Incorrect—Bandura (1997) argues that high self-efficacy produces higher levels of achievement.
  - *Correct*—Bandura (1997) argued that high self-efficacy produces higher levels of achievement.

- Use the *present tense* to express something that did not occur at a specific, definite time or an action beginning in the past and continuing to the present.
  - Incorrect—Since that result, investigators used the new method to increase self-efficacy.
  - *Correct*—Since that result, investigators use the new method to increase self-efficacy.

- Use the *past tense* to describe your results. (Hostility decreased significantly.)

- Use the *present tense* to discuss your results and to present conclusions. (The results of this experiment indicate that hostility . . .)

- *Agreement in number:* When a sentence contains the pronoun *they* or *their*, use a plural antecedent.
  - Incorrect—A teacher's sense of efficacy is grounded in their mastery experiences.
  - *Correct*—A teacher's sense of efficacy is grounded in his or her mastery experience.

- *Everyone* is singular—Everyone does his or her own work (*not* their own work). If the sentence gets awkward, make the subject plural—Students do their own work.

- Go on a "which hunt." Watch out for *which* when *that* is appropriate. Use *which* only if you can do without the clause that introduces it. In other words, a comma should always precede *which* when used to introduce a clause.

- Avoid using *since* when you mean *because*. *Since* implies a lapse of time.

- Avoid using *anxious* when you mean *eager*.

- If a paragraph goes on for nearly a page, it is too long. Find a place to break it.

- Don't use *while* when you mean *although* or *even though* or *whereas*. *While* implies concurrent time—happening together.

- Avoid split infinitives.
  - Incorrect—to empirically test
  - *Correct*—to test empirically

- The word *data* is plural.
  - Incorrect—The data supports his argument.
  - *Correct*—The data support his argument.

- Put statements in positive form.
  - Poor—He was not very punctual.
  - *Better*—He was usually late.

- Don't use *that* when referring to a person; *who* is correct.
  - Incorrect—The girl *that* came to dinner went home early.
  - *Correct*—The girl *who* came to dinner went home early.

This brief list of suggestions comes from a number of sources, including our colleagues Frank Pajares, Anita Woolfolk Hoy, and C. John Tarter. For a more extensive guide to writing, see the classic *Elements of Style* (Strunk & White, 2000). This is a *must* reading for all graduate students. We also recommend two other excellent books that will help students develop and hone their writing skills: *Gwynne's Grammar* by N. W. Gwynne and Steven Pinker's *The Sense of Style*.

Abduction is the process of studying a number of phenomena, observing their pattern, and formulating causal hypotheses.

Academic emphasis is the extent to which a school is driven by a quest for academic excellence—a press for academic achievement.

Academic optimism of a school is the collective belief of teachers that the faculty can teach, their students can learn, and parents are supportive; thus, teachers set high academic goals and press hard for achievement.

Alternative hypothesis states the direction of relation between the measures of the variables ($M_1 > M_2$).

ANOVA (analysis of variance) is a statistical procedure to determine whether the means of multiple groups are a likely function of chance.

Assumption is a statement that is taken for granted or accepted as true—that is, accepted without proof.

Beta weight is a regression weight, a coefficient of an independent variable in a multiple regression analysis, which indicates the strength of that variable in explaining the variance in the dependent variable, controlling for the effects of all the other independent variables in the regression; beta weights are typically standardized regression weights, and so they can be easily compared.

Between-group variance is a product of ANOVA and is the systematic variance produced by the independent variable; it is sometimes called **experimental variance.**

Categorical variable is one in which the values of the variable represent categories; it is an **in-kind variable** because the variation represents a category, not a numerical value.

Chi-square (χ^2) is the critical ratio that indicates how likely the relation between categorical variables departs from the chance model.

Coefficient of correlation (r) is a number that indicates the magnitude of the relation between two continuous variables such that the higher the absolute value of the correlation, the stronger the relation.

Collective efficacy is the perception of teachers in a school that the efforts of the faculty as a whole will have a positive effect on students.

Compound hypothesis is one that combines multiple hypotheses into a single hypothesis.

Concept is an abstract term that has been given a specific definition.

Conceptual definition explicates the construct by using other constructs and words to make the meaning clear; it is also called a **constitutive** or **theoretical definition.**

Constitutive definition explains the construct using other constructs, concepts, and words to make the meaning clear; it is also called a **conceptual** or **theoretical definition**.

Construct is a concept that typically has several dimensions.

Contingent hypothesis indicates that the conjecture depends on variation in some other variable (a moderator variable).

Continuous variable is one in which the values are ordered along a continuum; that is, the values represent the magnitude of the variation; they are also called **in-degree variables.**

Control variable is a variable related to the dependent variable, which must be taken into account either by design or by statistics to avoid being mistaken for the effect of the independent variable.

Custodial orientation is the view that students are irresponsible and undisciplined individuals who must be controlled by punitive and coercive action.

Deduction is a logical method of deriving specific predictions and hypotheses from a general set of assumptions, that is, moving from general premises to specific predictions and conclusions.

Dependent variable is the presumed effect or outcome of a relation.

Descriptive research is the process of simply describing relations without speculating about the cause.

Dogmatism is the structure of one's belief system; it deals with *how* one believes rather than *what* one believes.

Effect size is the magnitude or strength of the independent variable's influence on the dependent variable.

Elaboration of a variable is the explanation of the meaning of the numbers representing the variables.

Empirical is evidence based on observations, especially evidence obtained by systematic and controlled scientific research.

Enabling structure depicts a school where teachers believe that the organization works to support their teaching; organizational rules as well as administrative actions help the teachers rather than hinder their efforts.

Error variance is the variance left unexplained in an ANOVA; it is **within-group variance.**

Experimental research is systematic empirical inquiry in which the researcher introduces changes, notes effects, and has full control over the design of the study.

Experimental variance is the systematic variance produced by the manipulation of the independent variable of the study; it is the variance explained by the independent variable.

Ex post facto research, sometimes called **nonexperimental research**, is systematic empirical inquiry in which the researcher does not have direct control of the independent variable because the variable has already occurred.

Faculty trust in parents and students is the faculty's willingness to be vulnerable and work with parents and students based on the confidence that parents and students are serious partners who are benevolent, reliable, competent, honest, and open.

F value is a value computed using ANOVA; it is an index of the departure from the chance model.

Generalization is a statement or proposition that indicates the relation of two or more concepts or constructs.

Good hypothesis is declarative, clear, has at least two variables, and must be amenable to testing.

Humanistic orientation is the view that students learn by cooperative interaction and experience; self-discipline and self-regulation are goals rather than rigid and strict teacher control.

Hypothesis (hypotheses) is a conjectural statement that indicates the relation between key ideas or concepts.

Improvement science is a systematic form of action research that stresses a cycle of planning, doing, studying, and acting (PDSA).

In-degree variable represents the extent or degree of variation; it is also often called a **continuous variable.**

Independent variable is the presumed cause of a relation.

Induction is a logical method that moves from a series of observations in a variety of situations to a generalization that captures the general tendencies in the observations. In other words, a generalization is developed from a set of specific instances.

Inferential statistics is a mathematical way to see if the results of a study are likely a function of chance. Researchers use statistics and probability to reject the chance model and support their theoretical explanation.

In-kind variable is one in which the values represent categories not magnitude; for example, sex is an in-kind variable because the numbers represent the categories of male or female.

Intervening variable explains the relation between an independent and dependent variable.

Level of significance is the probability that the results are a function of chance.

Likert items indicate the extent of agreement with a statement (e.g., never, rarely, sometimes, often, always).

Manipulated variable is one that is controlled by the active intervention of a researcher in an experiment—that is, the experimental treatment.

Mean is the arithmetic average of some set of numbers.

Measured variable is an existing attribute that is measured by a scale or instrument.

Median is the middle score of a distribution of numbers.

Mediating variable (sometimes called an **intervening variable**) explains the relationship between the independent and dependent variables; it does not change the relation but explains it.

Method of authority is knowledge that is anchored in the statements of experts.

Method of intuition is knowledge built on assumptions that are obvious; knowledge is accepted as self-evident.

Method of science is systematic inquiry in which hypotheses are empirically tested in a controlled way.

Method of tenacity is a way of knowing where people hold to certain beliefs because they have always known these beliefs to be true—habit.

Mode is the most frequent number in a set of scores.

Moderating variable affects the direction and/or strength of the relation between an independent and a dependent variable.

Multiple correlation (R) indicates the magnitude or strength of the relation of a set of independent variables to one dependent variable.

Multiple regression is an extension of simple regression where there are multiple independent variables predicting a single dependent variable.

Negative correlation signifies that the independent and dependent variables vary in opposite directions—as one increases, the other decreases.

Nonexperimental research, sometimes called **ex post facto research**, is systematic empirical inquiry in which the researcher does not have direct control of the independent variable because the variable has already occurred.

Normal distribution is the bell-shaped curve that describes many naturally occurring physical and social phenomena, such as height and intelligence.

Null hypothesis is a statement that indicates that there is no relation between the measures of the variable ($M_1 = M_2$).

Objectivity is impartial judgment that rests outside an individual's personal preferences, biases, and wishes; it is agreement among knowledgeable judges of what is observed and what is done.

Objects are the persons, places, or things on which you conduct your research; the object of the study is also referred to as the **unit of analysis.**

Operational definition is a set of operations or behaviors that is used to measure a concept or construct.

Organizational science is the process of finding the basic principles that provide a general understanding of the structure and dynamics of organizational life.

PDSA Cycle is a continuous process of improving practice through planning, doing, studying, and acting.

Population (or universe) refers to all the elements of a set.

Positive correlation signifies that the independent and dependent variables covary: As one increases, so does the other.

Properties are the characteristics or attributes of an object.

p **Values** are numbers that indicate the probability that the result is a function of chance.

Qualitative research is inquiry based on the reported experiences of individuals through ethnographic analyses, fieldwork, or case studies; its purpose is in-depth understanding of social and human behavior in a specific context.

Quantitative research is scientific investigation that includes both experiments as well as other systematic methods that emphasize control and quantified measures of performance.

Range is the difference between the highest and lowest scores in a set of numbers, but it is also given as the span of scores beginning with the lowest score and ending with the highest score.

Reciprocal causation is a causal relation that flows in both directions; each variable causes the other.

Reflective inquiry is a method of science in which problems are defined, hypotheses are formulated to answer them, implications of the hypotheses are analyzed, and the hypotheses are tested in a systematic way.

Reliable measure is a consistent assessment of a concept.

Research hypothesis is a substantive statement describing the predicted relation between two or more concepts or variables— sometimes called a **theoretical hypothesis.**

Research problem is a question about the relation between two or more variables, which guides the research.

Sample is a subset of the population.

Science is a dynamic process of experimentation and observation that produces an interconnected set of principles that in turn generates further experimentation, observation, and refinement.

Scientific approach is a process of reflective inquiry, which is described in general as defining a problem, generating a hypothesis, analyzing the implications of the hypothesis, and testing the hypothesis.

Scientific research is systematic, controlled, empirical, and critical investigation of a set of hypotheses, also called theoretical research.

Self-efficacy is an individual's belief that he or she has the capacity to organize and execute the behavior to be successful in a particular situation.

Self-regulatory climate is an environment that supports and reinforces the psychological needs of autonomy, competence, and relatedness in students.

Specification of the hypothesis is a clear explication of how the variables of the hypothesis are related.

Standard deviation is the typical deviation from the mean for a set of scores; it is computed by subtracting the mean from each score in the set of numbers, squaring each deviation from the mean, summing the squared scores, dividing the sum by the number of scores in the set, and taking the square root of that number.

Standard score is derived by subtracting the mean from an individual raw score and then dividing that difference by the standard deviation.

Statistical hypothesis is stated in terms of the measures of the variables, that is, as a null or alternative hypothesis.

Substantive hypothesis is the statement of the hypothesis in conceptual or theoretical terms, sometimes called a **theoretical** or **research hypothesis.**

Systematic variance is produced by manipulation of the independent variable in a study; it is the variance due to the independent variable as computed by ANOVA; it is also called between-group variance or experimental variance.

Tautology is a statement that tells us nothing new, for example, if x, then x.

Theoretical definition describes the construct in terms of other constructs, concepts, and words to make the meaning clear; it is also called a **conceptual** or **constitutive** definition.

Theoretical hypothesis is the statement of the relation of two or more variables in concepts or words; it is also called a **substantive hypothesis** or **research hypothesis.**

Theory is a set of interrelated concepts, definitions, assumptions, and generalizations that systematically describes and explains regularities in behavior.

Theory of change is a conjectural explanation or model of change.

t Test is a statistical test to determine whether the difference between two means is likely a function of chance.

t Value is the value computed using a t test; it is an index of the departure from the chance model.

Unit of analysis is the object (person, place, or thing) on which you conduct your research.

Valid measure is one that captures the true meaning of a concept.

Value is a number that represents either the magnitude of the variable (e.g., an individual's height) or a category of the variable.

Variable is a property of an object that takes on different values as circumstances and situations change; the value may represent either the magnitude of the variable or a category of the variable.

Variance describes the variability *from the mean* of a set of measures.

Within-group variance is a product of ANOVA and is the variance due to chance and other unexplained conditions; it is sometimes called **error variance.**

z Score is a standard score that indicates how many standard deviations a score is above or below the mean.

REFERENCES

Adams, C. M. (2014). Collective student trust: A social resource for urban elementary students. *Educational Administration Quarterly, 50*, 135–159.

Adams, C. M., Forsyth, P. B., Dollarhide, E. A., Miskell, R. C., & Ware, J. K. (2015). Self-regulatory climate: A social resource for student regulation and achievement. *Teachers College Record, 117*(2).

Adams, C. M., Forsyth, P. B., Ware, J. K., Dollarhide, E. A., & Miskell, R. C. (2015, in press). Self-regulatory climate: A positive attribute of public schools. *Journal of Educational Research, 108*.

Adorno, T. W., Brunswick, E. F., Levinson, D. J., & Sanford, N. (1950). *The authoritarian personality*. New York, NY: Harper.

Alliance for Excellent Education. (2011). *A time for deeper learning: Preparing students for a changing world*. Retrieved from http://all4ed.org/wpcontent/uploads/2013/06/DeeperLearning.pdf

Altemeyer, B. (1996). *The authoritarian specter*. Cambridge, MA: Harvard University Press.

Appleton, J. J., Christenson, S. L., & Furlong, M. (2008). Student engagement with school: Critical conceptual and methodological issues of the construct. *Psychology in the Schools, 45*, 369–386.

Archambault, I., Janosz, M., Fallu, J. S., & Pagani, L. S. (2009). Student engagement and its relationship with early high school dropout. *Journal of Adolescence, 32*, 651–670.

Arrow, K. J. (1974). *The limits of organization*. New York, NY: Norton.

Ashton, P. T., & Webb, R. B. (1986). *Making a difference: Teachers' sense of efficacy and student achievement*. New York, NY: Longman.

Babbie, E. R. (1990). *Survey research methods* (2nd ed.). Belmont, CA: Wordsworth.

Baier, A. C. (1986). Trust and antitrust. *Ethics, 96*, 231–260.

Bandura, A. (1977). Self-efficacy: Toward a unifying theory of behavioral change. *Psychological Review, 84*, 191–215.

Bandura, A. (1986). *Social foundations of thought and action*. Englewood Cliffs, NJ: Prentice Hall.

Bandura, A. (1993). Perceived self-efficacy in cognitive development and functioning. *Educational Psychologist, 28*, 117–148.

Bandura, A. (1997). *Self-efficacy: The exercise of control*. New York, NY: Freeman.

Baron, R. M., & Kenny, D. A. (1986). The moderator-mediator variable distinction in social psychological research: Conceptual, strategic, and statistical considerations. *Journal of Personality and Social Psychology, 51*, 1173–1182.

Bass, B. M. (1998). *Transformational leadership: Industrial, military, and educational impact*. Mahwah, NJ: Lawrence Erlbaum.

Boghossian, P. (2006). *Fear of knowledge: Against relativism and constructivism*. New York, NY: Oxford University Press.

Bryk, A. S. (2009). Support a science of performance improvement. *The Phi Delta Kapan, 90*, 597–600.

Bryk, A. S., & Schneider, B. (2002). *Trust in schools: A core resource for improvement*. New York, NY: Russell Sage Foundation.

Buchler, J. (1955). *Philosophic writings of Peirce*. New York, NY: Dover.

Campbell, D. T. (1976). *Assessing the impact of planned social change*. Hanover, NH: The Public Affairs Center, Dartmouth College.

Carey, S., & Smith, C. (1993). On understanding the nature of scientific inquiry. *Educational Psychologist, 28*, 235–252.

Carlson, R. O. (1964). Environmental constraints and organizational consequences: The public school and its clients. In D. E. Griffiths (Ed.), *Behavioral science and educational administration* (pp. 262–276). Chicago, IL: University of Chicago Press.

Charters, W. W. (1992). *On understanding variables and hypotheses in scientific research*. Eugene, OR: Clearinghouse on Educational Management.

Checkland, P., & Holwell, S. (1998). Action research: Its nature and validity. *Systemic Practice and Action Research, 11*, 9–21.

Chirkov, V. I., & Ryan, M. R. (2001). Parent and teacher autonomy-support in Russian and U.S. adolescents: Common effects on well-being and academic motivation. *Journal of Cross-Cultural Psychology, 32*, 618–635.

Chow, B. (2010, October). The quest for deeper learning. *Education Week*. Retrieved from http://www.edweek.org/ew/articles/2010/10/06/06chow_ep.h30.html?intc=es

Coleman, J. S. (1961). *The adolescent society*. New York, NY: Free Press.

Coleman, J. S. (1985). Schools and the communities they serve. *Phi Delta Kappan, 66*, 527–532.

Coleman, J. S. (1987). Norms as social capital. In G. Radnitzky & P. Bernholz (Eds.), *Economic imperialism: The economic approach applied outside the field of economics* (pp. 133–155). New York, NY: Paragon House.

Conant, J. B. (1951). *Science and common sense*. New Haven, CT: Yale University Press.

Connell, J. P., & Klem, A. (2000). You can get there from here: Using a theory of change approach to plan urban education reform. *Journal of Educational and Psychological Consultation, 11*, 93–120.

Cronbach, L. J. (1971). Test validation. In R. L. Thorndike (Ed.), *Educational measurement* (pp. 443–507). Washington, DC: American Council on Education.

Deci, E. L., & Ryan, R. M. (1985). *Intrinsic motivation and self-determination in human behavior*. New York, NY: Plenum Press.

Deci, E., L., & Ryan, R. M. (2000). The "what" and "why" of goal pursuits: Human needs and the self-determination of behavior. *Psychological Inquiry, 11*, 227–268.

Deci, E. L., & Ryan, R. M. (2008). Self-Determination theory: A macrotheory of human motivation, development, and health. *Canadian Psychology, 49*, 182–185.

Deci, E. L., Vallerand, R. J., Pelletier, L. G., & Ryan, M. R. (1991). Motivation and education: the self-determination perspective. *Educational Psychologist, 26*, 325–346.

Deming, W. E. (2000). *The new economics for industry, government, education* (2nd ed.). Cambridge, MA: MIT Press.

Dewey, J. (1933). *How we think*. Mineola, NY: Dover.

Dubin, R. (1969). *Theory building*. New York, NY: Free Press.

Einstein, A., & Infield, L. (1966). *The evolution of physics*. New York, NY: Simon & Schuster.

Etzioni, A. (1962). *A comparative analysis of complex organizations*. New York, NY: Free Press.

Feigl, H. (1951). Principles and problems of theory construction in psychology. In W. Dennis (Ed.), *Current trends in psychological theory* (pp. 179–213). Pittsburgh, PA: University of Pittsburgh Press.

Fiedler, F. E. (1967). *A theory of leadership effectiveness*. New York, NY: McGraw-Hill.

Forsyth, P. B., Adams, C. M., & Hoy, W. K. (2011). *Collective trust: Why schools can't improve without it*. New York, NY: Teachers College Press.

Gilbert, D. C., & Levinson, D. J. (1957). Custodialism and humanism in mental hospital structure and staff ideology. In M. Greenblatt (Ed.), *The patient and the mental hospital* (pp. 20–34). Glencoe, IL: Free Press.

Goddard, R. G., Hoy, W. K., & Woolfolk Hoy, A. (2004). Collective efficacy: Theoretical development, empirical evidence, and future directions. *Educational Researcher, 33*, 3–13.

Goddard, R. G., LoGerfo, L., & Hoy, W. K. (2004). High

school accountability: The role of collective efficacy. *Educational Policy, 18*(30), 403–425.

Goddard, R. D., Sweetland, S. R., & Hoy, W. K. (2000). Academic emphasis of urban elementary schools and student achievement: A multi-level analysis. *Educational Administration Quarterly, 36,* 683–702.

Goddard, R. D., Tschannen-Moran, M., & Hoy, W. K. (2001). Teacher trust in students and parents: A multilevel examination of the distribution and effects of teacher trust in urban elementary schools. *Elementary School Journal, 102,* 3–17.

Gwynne, N. M. (2014). *Gwynne's grammar: The ultimate introduction to grammar and the writing of good English.* New York, NY: Alfred A. Knopf.

Hatch, T. (2006). *Into the classroom: Developing the scholarship of teaching and learning.* San Francisco, CA: Jossey-Bass.

Hays, W. L. (1994). *Statistics* (5th ed.). Fort Worth, TX: Harcourt Brace Jovanovich.

Henderson, J. E., & Hoy, W. K. (1982). Leader authenticity: The development and test of an operational measure. *Educational and Psychological Research, 3,* 63–75.

Higgins, E. T. (2004). Making theory useful: Lessons handed down. *Personality and Psychology Review, 8,* 138–145.

Honig, M. I., & Hatch, T. C. (2004). Crafting coherence: How schools strategically manage multiple, external demands. *Educational Researcher, 33,* 16–30.

Hoy, W. K. (1967). Organizational socialization: The student teacher and pupil control ideology. *Journal of Educational Research, 61,* 153–155.

Hoy, W. K. (1968). Pupil control and organizational socialization: The influence of experience on the beginning teacher. *School Review, 76,* 312–323.

Hoy, W. K. (1969). Pupil control ideology and organizational socialization: A further examination of the influence of experience on the beginning teacher. *School Review, 77,* 257–265.

Hoy, W. K. (1972). Dimensions of student alienation and characteristics of public high schools. *Interchange, 3,* 38–51.

Hoy, W. K. (2001). The pupil control studies: A historical, theoretical, and empirical analysis. *Journal of Educational Administration, 39,* 424–441.

Hoy, W. K. (2002). Faculty trust: A key to student achievement. *Journal of School Public Relations, 23*(2), 88–103.

Hoy, W. K. (2003). An analysis of enabling and mindful school structures: Some theoretical, research, and practical consideration. *Journal of Educational Administration, 41,* 87–108.

Hoy, W. K., & Hannum, J. (1997). Middle school climate: An empirical assessment of organizational health and student achievement. *Educational Administration Quarterly, 33,* 290–311.

Hoy, W. K., & Miskel, C. G. (2008). *Educational administration: Theory, research, and practice* (8th ed.). New York, NY: McGraw-Hill.

Hoy, W. K., & Miskel, C. G. (2013). *Educational administration: Theory, research, and practice* (9th ed.). New York, NY: McGraw-Hill.

Hoy, W. K., & Sabo, D. J. (1998). *Quality middle schools: Open and healthy.* Thousand Oaks, CA: Corwin Press.

Hoy, W. K., & Sweetland, S. R. (2000). Bureaucracies that work: Enabling not coercive. *Journal of School Leadership, 10,* 525–541.

Hoy, W. K., & Tarter, C. J. (1997). *The road to open and healthy schools: A handbook for change* (Elem. ed.). Thousand Oaks, CA: Corwin.

Hoy, W. K., & Tarter, C. J. (2008). *Administrators solving the problems of practice: Decision-making cases, concepts, and consequence* (3rd ed.). Boston, MA: Allyn & Bacon.

Hoy, W. K., Tarter, C. J., & Bliss, J. (1990). Organizational climate, school health, and effectiveness. *Educational Administration Quarterly, 26,* 260–279.

Hoy, W. K., Tarter, C. J., & Kottkamp, R. B. (1991). *Open schools/healthy schools: Measuring organizational climate*. Newbury Park, CA: Sage.

Hoy, W. K., Tarter, C. J., & Woolfolk Hoy, A. (2006a). Academic optimism of schools. In W. K. Hoy & C. Miskel (Eds.), *Contemporary issues in educational policy and school outcomes* (pp. 135–156). Greenwich, CT: Information Age.

Hoy, W. K., Tarter, C. J., & Woolfolk Hoy, A. (2006b). Academic optimism of schools: A force for student achievement. *American Educational Research Journal, 43*, 425–446.

Hoy, W. K., & Tschannen-Moran, M. (1999). Five faces of trust: An empirical confirmation in urban elementary schools. *Journal of School Leadership, 9*, 184–208.

Hoy, W. K., & Tschannen-Moran, M. (2003). The conceptualization and measurement of faculty trust in schools. In W. K. Hoy & C. Miskel (Eds.), *Studies in leading and organizing schools* (pp. 108–207). Greenwich, CT: Information Age.

Hoy, W. K., & Woolfolk, A. E. (1990). Socialization of student teachers. *American Educational Research Journal, 27*, 279–300.

Huber, M. T., & Hutchings, P. (2005). *The advancement of learning*. San Francisco, CA: Jossey-Bass.

Kenny, C. (2008). *The best practice: How the new quality movement is transforming medicine*. New York, NY: Public Affairs.

Kerlinger, F. N. (1979). *Behavioral research: A conceptual approach*. New York, NY: Holt, Rinehart, & Winston.

Kerlinger, F. N. (1986). *Foundations of behavioral research* (3rd ed.). New York, NY: Holt, Rinehart, & Winston.

Kerlinger, F. N., & Lee, H. B. (2000). *Foundations of behavioral research* (4th ed.). New York, NY: Wadsworth.

Keynes, J. M. (1936). *The general theory of employment, interest, and money*. London, England: Macmillan Press.

Klem, A. M., & Connell, J. P. (2004). Relationships matter: Linking teacher support to student engagement and achievement. *Journal of School Health, 74*, 262–273.

Langley, G. D., Moen, R. D., Nolan, K. M., Nolan, T. W., Norman, C. L., & Provost, L. P. (2010). *The improvement guide: A practical approach to enhancing organizational performance* (2nd ed.). San Francisco, CA: Jossey-Bass.

Lee, V. E., & Bryk, A. S. (1989). A multilevel model of the social distribution of high school achievement. *Sociology of Education, 62*, 172–192.

Leithwood, K. (1994). Leadership for school restructuring. *Educational Administration Quarterly, 30*, 498–518.

Lewin, K. (1946). Action research and minority problems. In G.W. Lewin (Ed.), *Resolving Social Conflicts* (pp. 34–46). New York, NY: Harper & Row.

Lewin, K. (1952). *Field theory in social science: Selected theoretical papers by Kurt Lewin*. London, England: Tavistock.

Lewin, K., Lippitt, R., & White, R. (1939). Patterns of aggressive behaviors in experimentally created social climates. *Journal of Social Psychology, 10*, 271–299.

Marks, H. M. (2000). Student engagement in instructional activity: Patterns in the elementary, middle, and high school years. *American Educational Research Journal, 37*, 153–184.

McDavid, J. C., & Hawthorn, L. R. L. (2006). *Program evaluation and performance measurement: An introduction to practice*. Thousand Oaks, CA: Sage.

McGuigan, L., & Hoy, W. K. (2006). Principal leadership: Creating a culture of academic optimism to improve achievement for all students. *Leadership and Policy in Schools, 5*, 203–229.

McKinley, W. (2010). Organizational theory development: Displacement of end. *Organizational Studies, 31*, 47–68.

Messick, S. (1995). Validity of psychological assessment; Validation of inferences from persons' responses and performances as scientific inquiry into school meaning. *American Psychologist, 50*(9), 741–749.

Miller, D. M. (2008). Data for school improvement and educational accountability: reliability and validity in practice. In K. Ryan & L. Shepard (Eds.), *The future of test-based educational accountability* (pp. 249–262). New York, NY: Routledge.

Mintzberg, H. (1989). *Mintzberg on management.* New York, NY: Free Press.

National Research Council, Division of Behavioral and Social Sciences and Education, Center for Education Research, Committee on Scientific Principles for Educational Research. (2002). *Scientific research in education* (R. J. Shavelson & L. Towne, Eds.). Washington, DC: National Academy Press.

Peirce, C. S. (1940). Abduction and induction. In J. Buchler (Ed.), *The philosophy of Peirce: Selected writings* (pp. 150–156). London, England: Routledge & Kegan Paul.

Peterson, C. (2000). The future of optimism. *American Psychologist, 55,* 44–55.

Pinker, S. (2014). *The sense of style: The thinking person's guide to writing in the 21st century.* New York, NY: Viking Press.

Proctor, R. W., & Capaldi, E. J. (2006). *Why science matters.* Maldin, MA: Blackwell.

Putnam, R. D. (1993). *Making democracy work: Civic traditions in modern Italy.* Princeton, NJ: Princeton University Press.

Rapoport, R. N. (1970). Three dilemmas in action research: With special reference to the Tavistock experience. *Human Relations, 23*(6), 499–513.

Reeve, J. (2002). Self-determination theory applied to educational settings. In E. Deci & R. Ryan (Eds.), *Handbook of self-determination research* (pp. 183–204). Rochester, NY: University of Rochester Press.

Reeve, J., Ryan, R., Deci, E. L., & Jang, H. (2008). Understanding and promoting autonomous self-regulation: A self-determination theory perspective. In D. H. Schunk & B. J. Zimmerman (Eds.), *Motivation and self-regulated learning: Theory, research, and applications* (pp. 223–244). New York, NY: Erlbaum.

Roberts, K. H., Hulin, C. L., & Rousseau, D. M. (1978). *Developing an interdisciplinary science of organizations.* San Francisco, CA: Jossey Bass.

Rokeach, M. (1960). *The open and closed mind.* New York, NY: Basic Books.

Ross, J. A. (1992). Teacher efficacy and the effects of coaching on student achievement. *Canadian Journal of Education, 17*(1), 51–65.

Ross, J. A. (1998). The antecedents and consequences of teacher efficacy. In J. Brophy (Ed.), *Advances in research on teaching* (Vol. 7, pp. 49–73). Greenwich, CT: JAI Press.

Rotter, J. (1954). *Social learning and clinical psychology.* Englewood Cliffs, NJ: Prentice Hall.

Seeman, M. (1959). On the meaning of alienation. *American Sociological Review, 34,* 783–791.

Snyder, C. R., Shorey, H. S., Cheavens, J., Pulvers, K. M., Adams, V. H., III, & Wiklund, C. (2002). Hope and academic success in college. *Journal of Educational Psychology, 94,* 820–826.

Spillane, J. P., Gomez, L. M., & Mesler, L. (2009). Notes on reframing the role of organizations in policy implementation: Resources for practice, in practice. In G. Sykes, B. Schneider, D. Plank, & T. Ford. (Eds.), *Handbook of education policy research* (pp. 409–425). New York, NY: Routledge.

Strunk, W., & White, E. B. (2000). *Elements of style* (4th ed.). New York, NY: Pearson.

Tosi, H. L. (2009). *Theories of organizations.* Thousands Oaks, CA: Sage.

Tsai, Y., Kunter, M., Ludtke, O., Trautwein, U., & Ryan, R. M. (2008). What makes lessons interesting? The role of situational and individual factors in three school subjects. *Journal of Educational Psychology, 100,* 460–472.

Tschannen-Moran, M., & Hoy, W. K. (2000). A multidisciplinary analysis of the nature, meaning, and measurement of trust. *Review of Educational Research, 70,* 547–593.

Waller, W. (1932). *The sociology of teaching*. New York, NY: Wiley.

Willower, D. J. (1975). Theory in educational administration. *Journal of Educational Administration, 13,* 77–91.

Willower, D. J., & Jones, R. G. (1967). Control in an educational organization. In J. D. Raths, J. R.

Pancella, & J. S. Van Ness (Eds.), *Studying teaching* (pp. 424–428). Englewood Cliffs, NJ: Prentice Hall.

Wood, R., & Bandura, A. (1989). Social cognitive theory of organizational management. *Academy of Management Review, 14,* 361–384.

Wright, J., (2013). *Explaining science's success: Understanding how scientific knowledge works*. Bristol, CT: Acumen.

AUTHOR INDEX

SUBJECT INDEX

ABOUT THE AUTHORS

Wayne K. Hoy received his B.S. from Lock Haven State College in 1959 and then taught mathematics at Cheltenham High School in Pennsylvania. He received his D.Ed. from The Pennsylvania State University in 1965 and began his professorial career at Oklahoma State University. He moved to Rutgers University in 1968, where he was a distinguished professor, department chair, and Associate Dean for Academic Affairs. In 1994, he joined the faculty at The Ohio State University as an endowed professor, The Novice G. Fawcett Chair in Educational Administration. In January of 2013, he retired and is now a professor emeritus at The Ohio State University. Over his career, he has received numerous acknowledgments and awards: In 1973, he received the Lindback Foundation Award for Distinguished Teaching from Rutgers University; in 1987, he received the Alumni Award for Professional Research from the Rutgers University Graduate School of Education; in 1991, he received the Excellence in Education Award from The Pennsylvania State University; in 1992, he received the Meritorious Research Award from the Eastern Educational Research Association; in 1996, he became an alumni fellow of The Pennsylvania State University; and in 2001 he received the Research Award from the Ohio State College of Education. He is past secretary-treasurer of the National Conference of Professors of Educational Administration (NCPEA) and past president of the University Council for Educational Administration (UCEA). In November 2003, he received the Roald Campbell Lifetime Achievement Award in Educational Administration and in 2009 he was elected a Fellow of the American Educational Research Association. He is the author, coauthor, or coeditor of 24 books in the fields of research and theory, educational administration, decision making, leadership, and instructional supervision. Three of his recent books are *Instructional Leadership: A Research-based Guide to Learning in Schools* (2013), written with his wife Anita Woolfolk Hoy; *Educational Administration: Theory, Research and Practice* (2013), coauthored with Cecil Miskel; and *Improving Instruction Through Supervision, Evaluation, and Professional Development* (2014), with Michael DiPaola.

Curt M. Adams is an associate professor of educational leadership and policy studies at the University of Oklahoma and co-director of the Oklahoma Center for Educational Policy. In 2014, he was awarded the Linda Clarke Anderson Presidential Professorship for outstanding contribution to the University, field, and community through research, teaching, and service. He conducts research on the social-psychology of school systems, performance measurement, accountability, and improvement science. He is past founder and director of the San Miguel School of Tulsa, a nonprofit, gratuitous school based on the Lasallian charism of serving socially deprived students and families. Recent publications include: Self-regulatory Climate: A Positive Attribute of Schools (*Journal of Educational Research*); Self-regulatory Climate: A Social Resource for Student Regulation and Achievement (*Teachers College Record*); Revisiting the Collective Trust Effect in Urban Elementary Schools (*Educational Administration Quarterly*); Collective Trust: A Social Indicator of Instructional Capacity (*Journal of Educational Administration*); Parent Social Networks and Parent Responsibility: Implications for School Leadership (*Journal of School Leadership*); and Collective Trust: Why Schools Can't Improve Without It (*Teachers College Press*).